THE HEALING FOUNTAIN

Writings Selected from Contemporary Christians

THE HEALING FOUNTAIN

Writings Selected from Contemporary Christians

Edited by Betty Thompson

Cover design and photographs by John P. Taylor

THE HEALING FOUNTAIN

Education and Cultivation Division,
Board of Global Ministries, United Methodist Church,
475 Riverside Drive, New York, N.Y. 10027

Library of Congress Catalog Card Number 73-76166

Format by Roger C. Sadler and Karen E. Tureck

ACKNOWLEDGEMENTS

The author wishes to acknowledge with most sincere thanks the permissions, granted by publishers, authors, or agents, to reprint the copyrighted materials in this book.

Most of the selections chosen are protected by copyright and may not be reproduced in any form without the consent of the copyright owner: publisher, author, or agent. Since the Copyright Page cannot accommodate all acknowledgements and copyright notices, this, and following pages, shall constitute an extension of the Copyright Page for acknowledgements to:

ABINGDON PRESS for *The Message and the Messengers,* by D. T. Niles, pp. 26-28. Copyright © 1966 by The Abingdon Press; *and* **Songs from the Slums** by Toyohiko Kagawa, pp. 40-42, 46-48. Copyright renewal 1963 by Lois J. Erickson. Reprinted by permission of The Abingdon Press.

ASSOCIATION PRESS for **The Substance of Faith and Other Cotton Patch Sermons** by Clarence Jordan (pp. 73, 75, 76, 77). Copyright © 1972 by Florence Jordan, published by Association Press. Reprinted by permission of Association Press.

right 1955 by Paul Tillich. Reprinted by permission of Charles Scribner's Sons.

THE SEABURY PRESS, INC. *for* **The Alphabet of Grace,** by Frederick Buechner, pp. 3, 4, 8, 13, 43-46. © 1970 by Frederick Buechner; *and* **The Magnificent Defeat,** Frederick Buechner, pp. 47-50, 105, 129-130. Copyright © 1966 by The Seabury Press, Inc. Used by permission of The Seabury Press.

THE WESTMINSTER PRESS, *for* **I Believe in the Living God** by Emil Brunner, John Holden translator-ed., pp. 90-93. Copyright © MCMLXI, W. L. Jenkins, The Westminster Press; *and* **Free Men** by Suzanne de Dietrich, trans. by Olive Wyon, pp. 17, 42, 43, 45, 46, 51-52, 100-101, 105. Published by The Westminster Press, Philadelphia, 1961. Copyright © 1961, SCM Press, Ltd. Used by permission.

THE WORLD PUBLISHING CO. *for* **Leaves from the Notebooks of a Tamed Cynic** by Reinhold Niebuhr, pp. 45-46, 74, 175, 216-217. Copyright © 1929 by Reinhold Niebuhr. Reprinted by permission of The World Publishing Co.

YALE UNIVERSITY PRESS, *for* **The Courage to Be,** Paul Tillich, pp. 171-172, 180-181. Copyright 1952 by Yale University Press. Used by permission of Yale University Press.

ADDITIONAL ACKNOWLEDGEMENTS

"The Time My Father Died," Joseph W. Mathews, pp. 9-11, *Motive,* Jan.-Feb., 1964. Used by permission of The Ecumenical Institute and quoted from their leaflet.

"How Do You Want to Die?" Claude H. Thompson, *Christian Advocate,* February 17, 1972. Used by permission of Sue L. Thompson (Mrs. Claude H.).

"Tomorrow: Moderator Suzuki's Last Message," *Kyodan Times,* July 19, 1969. Used by permission of Sakae Suzuki (Mrs. Masahisa Suzuki).

"Nobel Prize Acceptance Speech," Martin Luther King, Jr., *New York Times,* December 11, 1964. Copyright © The Nobel Foundation, 1965. Used by permission of The Nobel Foundation, Stockholm.

"Pilgrimage to Non-Violence," Martin Luther King, Jr., *Christian Century,* Apr. 13, 1960. Used by permission of Joan Daves for Martin Luther King Estate.

"Most Durable Power," Martin Luther King, Jr., *Christian Century,* June 5, 1957. Used by permission of Joan Daves for Martin Luther King Estate.

"Suffering and Faith," Martin Luther King, Jr., *Christian Century,* April 27, 1960; used by permission of Joan Daves for Martin Luther King Estate.

"New Sense of Direction," Martin Luther King, Jr., *Worldview*, April, 1972, vol. XV, No. 4. Reprinted with the permission of *Worldview*, 170 East 64 Street, New York, N.Y.

"Thy Kingdom Come: Christian Hope in the Modern World" (Proceedings of 1962 Liturgical Week). Used by permission of The Liturgical Conference; in *They Call Us Dead Men,* Daniel Berrigan, pp. 60-61.

This book follows the spelling and punctuation of the sources quoted; therefore there are minor inconsistencies in style.

CONTENTS

In the deserts of the heart
Let the healing fountain start,
In the prison of his days
Teach the free man how to praise.

W. H. Auden

INTRODUCTION

It wasn't easy. I confess I was attracted to this project because I thought it would be. When I first heard such a book suggested, it appealed to me immensely. What could be more delightful than to make a collection of contemporary Christian writers which would introduce one's own favorites to others? An upcoming sabbatical would provide the time, and I would roam through favorite authors and compile a kind of collection of contemporary piety, a sampling of twentieth century men and women whose lives were grounded in faith. Of course, there would be Bonhoeffer, the heroic German Christian whose martyr's life had demonstrated his concept of the church for others. And, Martin Luther King, true apostle of non-violence. But not only martyrs, for this was a book which must appeal to ordinary Christians whose witness while often heroic usually does not exact the life itself to verify its authenticity. There must be those whose message would apply to what poet Randall Jarrell has called "the dailiness of life." And the book must speak of life and death, community and celebration, the individual's quest for God and those areas where God is at work in the world.

In short, it was, I found, to deal with everything. For everywoman. For this was to be a study book for United Methodist women who were used to rigorous Bible study. It must be concrete and while it would deal with the abstract, it should not use terms which were too theological. It should be a book which could be read by an individual, and it should not have too much interpretation in the way of the speakers and those to whom they were speaking. It was to be a book which would stimulate discussion for groups and lead them to look further into the works of the authors presented and into their own lives. Its bias would be towards those writers whose lives were both contemplative and active for it comes at a time when an artificial split between individual and corporate concepts of salvation is polarizing the church. Here one, I hoped, might find together the horizontal and vertical dimensions of faith, the immanent and the transcendent, the finite and the infinite, the flesh and the spirit.

The collection would present twentieth century men and women, black and white, Roman Catholic and Protestant, professional theologian and monk, lay woman and priest whose spiritual quest took them into the world. And it would present them not in longer essays but in brief passages — from books, letters, diaries, a poem or a song. It still sounded if not easy, enjoyable.

My methodology was autobiographical. I began re-reading those books on my shelves which had meant much to me, recalling and seeking out others I had wanted to read but hadn't. I sent out a flock of letters to friends in various parts of the world and asked them for suggestions. Some dutifully replied, some joyfully, some not at all. One wiser than the rest said, "Ah, I'm not going to write that book for you," but nonetheless made suggestions included herein. I took the liberty of including old friends like Janet Lacey, the English woman whose compassion and imagination grew into the remarkable success of Britain's Christian Aid, and D. T. Niles, Asian Christian who had been my colleague in the years when we both worked for the World Council of Churches and whose Bible studies always spoke lucidly and boldly of his evangelical faith. There were others, whom I had the privilege of meeting in my work as an ecumenical journalist, like Roger Schutz, the prior of Taizé, the Protestant brotherhood in France, where I spent a memorable Easter week-end in the mid-fifties. The quiet of the five a.m. service in the little Burgundian village, the memory of Martin Luther King addressing the marchers in Montgomery, a novelist I met at a party when I first came to New York — all these moments were there waiting to be recalled.

And although Roger Schutz and Martin Luther King were naturals for such a book I probably would not have included the novelist Frederick Buechner if another friend, Theodore A. Gill, had not suggested that I read two of his provocative devotional books — The Alphabet of Grace and The Magnificent Defeat. John Garrett of the Pacific Theological School

12

in Fiji reminded me to take another look (I had never taken the first) at the almost forgotten poetry which the great Japanese Christian Kagawa had written out of his loneliness as a young man working in the slums of Tokyo. J. Robert Nelson of Boston University School of Theology suggested the passage about the chestnut tree from another German Christian martyr Paul Schneider. One thing led to another. Now the problem was where to stop.

I continued to buy books and my faithful secretary Kiku Kam pursued others in the libraries of United Mission Library (Methodist-Presbyterian), Union Theological Seminary, and Columbia University. Some days I wanted to put in too much. On others I felt I would never have enough or know how to organize what I had. Then some marvelous new thing would come. A missionary-journalist friend, James Stentzel sent the deathbed letters (from tapes) of Japanese church moderator, Suzuki. Alva I. Cox, Jr., shared with me his television scripts on Karl Barth, Dietrich Bonhoeffer, Paul Tillich, and Reinhold Niebuhr.

And then about midway I discovered some other books much like what I was trying to do. I particularly liked one called *Who Am I?* by Lowell D. Streiker (Sheed and Ward) who included many of the persons and passages I was planning to use but was more adventurous in that he had many other than Christians (Malcolm X, Martin Buber, Henry Miller). I read two books by Elizabeth O'Connor *The Sound of Silence* (Word Publications, Waco, Texas), and *Our Many Selves: A Handbook for Self Discovery* (Harper & Row), and admired her excerpts and exercises. Thomas Weiser's collection *Salvation Today and Contemporary Experience* prepared for the World Council of Churches was again far more adventurous in using sources outside the Christian faith to call attention to those places in the world crying for salvation today (World Council of Churches, available early in 1973).

But I was committed to this collection so I continued to read and amass far more than I could use. Editor Frances Eshelman and colleague Mary Lou Van Buren of the Women's Division of the United Methodist Board of Global Ministries made many helpful suggestions of sources and helped in the painful task of cutting.

So here it is. Be warned that some of the categories are arbitrary. You may find that one passage contradicts another. For the opinions of man, God, the world, the church are many. The selection, as I have warned, is highly personal and made because I am who I am. My hope is that readers will find things here which will stimulate their own thoughts, prayers, lives.

I wish you the joy of discovering not only the writers here but of making your own collection. And for those of you who find the book satisfying and stimulating, I have another one made up of all the things which I had so painfully to excise at the time when my labor was wrested from me.

Betty Thompson

March, 1973

FAITH, HOPE, LOVE

1

FAITH, HOPE, LOVE

FAITH, HOPE, LOVE

Faith, hope, and love are foundations of the Christian life. These are the sources for our Witness, our attitudes toward Life and Death, the Church and the World, and what we celebrate: our Joy, Freedom, and Peace. One could easily argue for another arrangement. Witness could be placed first: the embodiment of the faith, hope, and love. It might be useful for readers as they progress in the study of this book to make their own categories and arrangements. In this section appear some of the great theologians of our time: Karl Barth, Emil Brunner, Reinhold Niebuhr, and Paul Tillich. Barth and Brunner are Swiss of the Reformed tradition. Reinhold Niebuhr began his mission in the Evangelical Church, a small American church of German speaking origin whose heirs belong to the United Church of Christ. Paul Tillich, the great German theologian, spent the latter part of his life in America after he fled the Nazis. These are men who spent most of their lives teaching seminarians and writing theological works. But they were also much concerned with their times. They followed Karl Barth's advice to read the Bible in one hand and the newspaper in the other. They were also preachers. Reinhold Niebuhr's ministry as a young man was in the city of Detroit, and it was there that he got caught up in the labor and race problems of his day. Until the end of his life Karl Barth visited the prisoners and preached the Gospel to them in his home town of Basel, Switzerland. Tillich's sermons, many of them preached to young men and women at Union Seminary, are as clear as his more systematic theology was sometimes abstract. Brunner also is a powerful preacher. Embodied theology is the emphasis throughout this volume. Because theologians have often spoken in the jargon of their particular discipline, there is resentment against them on the part of many ordinary people. The theologians represented here are chosen because they were able to speak to us powerfully, especially in their lives, sermons, and diaries. Some of the great names of the immediate past are here because they have helpful lessons we have not yet learned. Theology, says Frederick Buechner, the American novelist who is also a Presbyterian minister, is mostly autobiography. Their theology—or simply stated what they think about God—came out of their experiences as human beings as well as their impressive scholarship.

The great martyrs and witnesses like Martin Luther King, the American advocate of nonviolence, and Dietrich Bonhoeffer, the gentle German who was hanged for his participation in a plot to take Hitler's life and end the war, are included in this section as well as under "Witness" for it is their faith that sustained them in their witness. The English woman, Florence Allshorn, whose devotion to community and prayer grew out of her unhappy experiences as a young missionary, belongs here along with another great woman missionary of our time, the Yugoslav peasant, Mother Teresa, whose Home for the Destitute and Dying in India made such an indelible impression on the veteran journalist and former editor of *Punch,* the British humor magazine, Malcolm Muggeridge. Mother Teresa's work is something which I have been privileged to see in action. The sights and sounds of that place where the broken and dying, young and old of Calcutta are brought to be tended with love and dignity are unforgettable. The great missionary doctor, musician, and philosopher Albert Schweitzer is represented by a passage from his early book *In Quest of the Historical Jesus.*

Kagawa, the Japanese Christian who lived a lonely life in the slums and forged the social conscience of the tiny Christian church in Japan, is unjustly forgotten by our generation.

Two Roman Catholic priests are here: one the Jesuit Daniel Berrigan whose opposition to the Vietnam war landed him in Danbury Prison, and the other the talkative (in his poems and books) Trappist Thomas Merton who was killed in an accident in Bangkok in 1968. Thomas Merton wrote about his early conversion in the book, *The Seven Storey Mountain.*

Roger Schutz is the prior of the famous Protestant brotherhood of Taizé, in France. While many of the movements of the post-World War II world seem to have run their course, Taizé, whose brothers now number seventy and who work in many places, has awakened the interest of this generation of young people. Thousands go at Easter and other times of the year to the little village atop a hill in Burgundy where they discuss the problems of the Third World and seek to learn some of the intimacy these Taizé brothers have with the living God.

Dag Hammarskjöld, the Swedish secretary general of the United Nations who died in a plane crash in Africa, left a diary of spiritual discovery which was published after his death. Many of his secular friends found these revelations quite shocking, for the Swedish diplomat was largely silent in his witness when it came to direct articulation of his feelings about his faith. That this belief very much informed his decisions and his work will be obvious to any reader of his mystical *Markings*.

So here they are—some famous and some of whom you may have never heard: Men and women of our time whose lives were grounded in the hope that is Jesus Christ.

Some will also appear in other parts of the book, but if you would know more of them, there are riches to be sought out both in their writing and the story of their days lived and being lived in faith, hope, and love.

WE WERE MADE TO LOVE

We had not understood what the love of God is. We had not believed so much of the love of God; that it is not only in the good-will, as of a Father to his sons, which God has to all creatures; not only man's filial looking to Him and love; but that it is the strongest of all things, the very movement and generation of God Himself.

His creatures must always be desirous, because the flame of His desire entered into them, at their creation. It is their energy and elation. If they go God's way satisfying their desire as He satisfied His own, in Love, His kind of Love, they go the way of Fate and share the Eternal life. But if they let go of Love, they let go of eternal life and go out where darkness and death are and have nothing but anxious and unsatisfied desires (Jacob Boehme).

If God is love and we were made to love as the stars were made to shine, then every creature is desirous of finding this disinterested Love—the spirit is the flame of this disinterested love—and all the unhappiness, the struggle to make oneself felt, anger, self-assertion, divisions and contentions, dryness and depression are only the desire robbed of love; a beat against the wind—defeat, and therefore unhappiness, unease, no serenity and no peace. It is this desire—God-given—wandering from its course towards itself that is the cause of our exclusion from the heavenly light. How can lovelessness live with God? Besides, because it will not go God's way and cannot enter into eternal life, which is the spirit's fate, it slowly becomes degraded, thickened, so that we come to the place where all this truth seems very high-falutin' and something possible to by-pass. And that is its tragedy, that it had an old will to love but that it has let go of Love.

But Love was not meant to die. It is the fire and energy of the Spirit. We wonder why we grow discouraged and flat, why there is so little spiritual force in us, why life seems dry, why we get on so slowly and fail so often, and God doesn't seem to help. If only we could give the desire for self away into something outside ourselves, greater than ourselves, then our spirit would kindle at it, love and burn with ever-renewing life; we should discover that we were alive and happy in a new way—because we had found our true nature and we were poised from a steady centre. We had found eternal life, God's own way to love.

FLORENCE ALLSHORN

IT CONQUERS THE WORLD

The love for equals is a human thing—of friend for friend, brother for brother. It is to love what is loving and lovely. The world smiles.

The love for the less fortunate is a beautiful thing—the love for those who suffer, for those who are poor, the sick, the failures, the unlovely. This is compassion, and it touches the heart of the world.

The love for the more fortunate is a rare thing—to love those who succeed where we fail, to rejoice without envy with those who rejoice, the love of the poor for the rich, of the black man for the white man. The world is always bewildered by its saints.

And then there is the love for the enemy—love for the one who does not love you but mocks, threatens, and inflicts pain. The tortured's love for the torturer. This is God's love. It conquers the world.

FREDERICK BUECHNER

THE MOST DURABLE POWER

I still believe that love is the most durable power in the world. Over the centuries men have sought to discover the highest good. This has been the chief quest of ethical philosophy. . . . What is the summum bonum of life? . . . It is love. This principle stands at the center of the cosmos. As John says, "God is love." He who loves is a participant in the being of God. He who hates does not know God.

MARTIN LUTHER KING, JR.

MORNING PRAYERS

O God, early in the morning I cry to thee.
Help me to pray
And to concentrate my thoughts to thee;
I cannot do this alone.

In me there is darkness.
But with thee there is light;
I am lonely, but thou leavest me not;
I am feeble in heart, but with thee there is help;
I am restless, but with thee there is peace.
In me there is bitterness, but with thee there is patience;
I do not understand thy ways,
But thou knowest the way for me.

O heavenly Father,
I praise and thank thee
For the peace of the night;
I praise and thank thee for this new day;
I praise and thank thee for all thy goodness
and faithfulness throughout my life.

Thou hast granted me many blessings;
Now let me also accept what is hard
from thy hand.
Thou wilt lay on me no more
than I can bear.
Thou makest all things work together for good
for thy children.

Lord Jesus Christ
Thou wast poor
and in distress, a captive and forsaken as I am.
Thou knowest all man's troubles;
Thou abidest with me
when all men fail me;
Thou rememberest and seekest me;
It is thy will that I should know thee
and turn to thee.
Lord, I hear thy call and follow;
Do thou help me.

O Holy Spirit,
Give me faith that will protect me
from despair, from passions, and from vice;
Give me such love for God and men
as will blot out all hatred and bitterness;
Give me the hope that will deliver me
from fear and faint-heartedness.

O holy and merciful God,
my Creator and Redeemer,
my Judge and Saviour,
Thou knowest me and all that I do.
Thou dost hate and punish evil without respect of persons
in this world and the next;
Thou forgivest the sins of those
who sincerely pray for forgiveness;
Thou lovest goodness, and rewardest it on this earth
with a clear conscience.
and, in the world to come,
with a crown of righteousness.

I remember in thy presence all my loved ones,
my fellow-prisoners, and all who in this house
perform their hard service;
Lord, have mercy.
Restore me to liberty,
and enable me so to live now
that I may answer before thee and before men.
Lord, whatever this day may bring,
Thy name be praised.
Amen.
DIETRICH BONHOEFFER

CHRIST TRANSFORMS

Little by little Christ transforms and transfigures in us all rebellious contradictory tendencies, all those troubled states
of mind and vexed moments which are still left in the depth of
our personalities and over which the will sometimes has no
control.

It is possible from now on to assure certain people who are convinced that they have 'ruined their lives', that in the patience of God nothing is lost. Christians as eminent as St. John of the Cross and St. Teresa of Avila began fairly late to live a new life—two saints who have led so many men and women to Christ and who then speak of the fire kindled with all the wood of their past.

For those who are marked by suffering and by the Cross of Christ, the day will come when they will be able to burn with the fire which is fed by all their past. From that moment they will know that nothing exists without a reason for it— nothing is ever lost in God.

The light of Christ transfigures in us the shadows themselves. These shadows are nonetheless present and sometimes we can do nothing about them. But then it happens that as the life of Christ slowly develops in us, what was still dark, restless, opaque and even disturbing is peacefully enlightened and taken up into God. Nothing is lost on this earth because God is strong enough to give us back all things, reshaped, changed, revitalized, transfigured by him. However, we do have to wish to turn ourselves towards the light.

Just as the light of Christ does its work in the midst of our inner darkness it also works on the opacity of the world. So God adopts to himself unbelieving humanity; by living in the midst of human beings who cannot believe a Christian is a Christ-bearer; with the utmost discretion he communicates the very presence of God.

The apostles contemplate Christ transfigured and they wish to live in this dazzling light because they know very well that they are living then a climax of their lives. But they have to come down from the mountain and from then on to see the light of Christ shining in the growing Church, in themselves, in the world in the midst of men.

And that is also true for each Christian; he must come back down and radiate the glory of God without noisy words in such a way that, by this light of Christ in us, everyone will have an insight into the very source of our visible unity. By it the man who is not able to believe, without knowing how, will be led towards hope in God.

ROGER SCHUTZ

THE COURAGE TO BE

The divine self-affirmation is the power that makes the self-affirmation of the finite being, the courage to be, possible. Only because being-itself has the character of self-affirmation in spite of nonbeing is courage possible. Courage participates in the self-affirmation of being-itself, it participates in the power of being which prevails against nonbeing. He who receives this power in an act of mystical or personal or absolute faith is aware of the source of his courage to be.

Man is not necessarily aware of this source. In situations of cynicism and indifference he is not aware of it. But it works in him as long as he maintains the courage to take his anxiety upon himself. In the act of the courage to be the power of being is effective in us, whether we recognize it or not. Every act of courage is a manifestation of the ground of being, however questionable the content of the act may be. The content may hide or distort true being, the courage in it reveals true being, not arguments but the courage to be reveals the true nature of being-itself. By affirming our being we participate in the self-affirmation of being-itself. There are no valid arguments for the "existence" of God, but there are acts of courage in which we affirm the power of being, whether we know it or not. If we know it, we accept consciously. If we do not know it, we nevertheless accept it and participate in it. And in our acceptance of that which we do not know the power of being is manifest to us. Courage has revealing power, the courage to be is the key to being itself.

PAUL TILLICH

FAITH IS PERSONAL

Accompanying Mother Teresa, as we did, to these different activities for the purpose of filming them - to the Home for the Dying, to the lepers and unwanted children, I found I went through three phases. The first was horror mixed with pity, the second compassion pure and simple, and the third, reaching far beyond compassion, something I had never experienced before - an awareness that these dying and derelict men and women, these lepers with stumps instead of hands, these unwanted children, were not pitiable, repulsive or forlorn, but rather dear and delightful; as it might be, friends of long standing, brothers and sisters. How is it to be explained - the very heart and mystery of the Christian faith? To soothe those battered old heads, to grasp those poor stumps, to take in one's arms those children consigned to dustbins, because it is his head, as they are his stump and his children, of whom he said that whosoever received one such child in his name received him.

During the period of our filming I went each morning to Mass with the Sisters. One of them was always posted to let me in, and in the chapel there was a place beside Mother Teresa for me, and a missal opened at the correct page. I felt perfectly content to be worshipping with them, even though I could not, and had no wish to, partake of the Sacraments. For Mother Teresa, faith is a personal relationship with God and the incarnate Christ; the Mass (Communion) the spiritual food which sustains her, without which, as she told me, she could not get through one single day or hour of the life of dedication she has chosen; the Church something she belongs to, serves and obeys as revealing and fulfilling God's purposes on earth. The various controversies and conflicts now shaking the Church scarcely touch her; they will pass, she says, and the Church will remain to perform its divinely inspired and directed function.

MALCOLM MUGGERIDGE

READ WITH OPEN EYES

The "great" commitment is so much easier than the ordinary everyday one—and can all too easily shut our hearts to the latter. A willingness to make the ultimate sacrifice can be associated with, and even produce, a great hardness of heart.

You thought you were indifferent to praise for achievements which you would not yourself have counted to your credit, or that, if you should be tempted to feel flattered, you would always remember that the praise far exceeded what the events justified. You thought yourself indifferent—until you felt your jealousy flare up at his naive attempts to "make himself important," and your self-conceit stood exposed.

Concerning the hardness of heart — and its littleness — let me read with open eyes the book my days are writing — and learn.

DAG HAMMARSKJÖLD

GOD'S VOICE MADE ARTICULATE

Never was a book so full of incredible sayings—everywhere the sense of mystery dominates; unless you feel that mystery, all becomes prosaic—nothing about God is prosaic.

The Word was God. Short, strange sentence not easy to be trite about and think you know. The wind bloweth where it listeth, so is everyone who is born of the spirit—what room for heaviness and lethargy, drift and complacency there? I am the Door—into what unimaginable beauty? I speak that which I have seen with My Father—no wonder men didn't understand His words. God's voice at last made purely articulate to creatures of earth and time, with ears so insensitive; but if they are the living words of God who created us, they *are* spirit and they *are* life as He said . . . .

FLORENCE ALLSHORN

CHRISTIANITY STANDS BEYOND TRAGEDY

Evil is not a part of God, nor yet a part of essential man. This Saviour is a revelation of the goodness of God and the essential goodness of man, *i.e.,* the second Adam. He is indeed defeated in history but in that very defeat proves that he cannot be ultimately defeated. That is, he reveals that it is God's nature to swallow up evil in Himself and destroy it. Life in its deepest essence is not only good but capable of destroying the evil which has been produced in it. Life is thus not at war with itself. Its energy is not in conflict with its order. Hence the Saviour truly says: "Weep not for me." Christianity stands beyond tragedy. If there are tears for this man on the cross they cannot be tears of "pity and terror." The cross does not reveal life at cross purposes with itself. On the contrary, it declares that what seems to be an inherent defect in life itself is really a contingent defect in the soul of each man, the defect of the sin which he commits in his freedom. If he can realize that fact, if he can weep for himself, if he can repent, he can also be saved. He can be saved by hope and faith. His hope and faith will separate the character of life in its essential reality from life as it is revealed in sinful history.

This man on the cross who can say "Weep not for me" is also able to save us from our tears of self-pity. What he reveals about life transmutes tears of self-pity into tears of remorse and repentance. Repentance does not accuse life or God but accuses self. In that self-accusation lies the beginning of hope and salvation. If the defect lies in us and not in the character of life, life is not hopeless.If we can only weep for ourselves as men we need not weep for ourselves as man.

REINHOLD NIEBUHR

EASTER CERTAINTY

Inseparably sin, anxiety, and hopelessness belong together on the one side, and faith, peace, and hope on the other side. We can be redeemed from hopelessness and born anew to a living hope only by being redeemed from godlessness and reconciled and united anew with God. The Easter message belongs together with the message of Good Friday. The gospel of Jesus Christ is not put together from many pieces; it is, as John very meaningfully says of the garment of Jesus, from one piece without a seam. Only he who beforehand has been reconciled to God can really believe in the Easter message, so that it becomes a living hope. One cannot deal directly with hopelessness and anxiety about death but only in such a way that one deals with the basis of it. It stems from a disturbed relationship with God; it can only be removed if the relation to God is restored, if we are reconciled to God and are at peace with him through the cross of Jesus Christ. See, that is why it does not help much if one simply believes in the resurrection record of the Gospels, what one calls believing in such case. Among the many millions who have from their childhood believed and never doubted it, there are also many millions in whose life this so-called faith in the resurrection means nothing at all. Their faith is simply a piece of their world picture; they believe that Jesus is raised from the dead, as they believed that earlier lake dwellers lived in our land or that the earth is a ball. Despite this faith in the Easter event, they suffer just as others from anxiety about life, and fight, just as those who believe nothing, brutally and greedily from the door-closing panic for their place in life. Why? Just because they are not reconciled to God, because this Easter faith does not come from the experience of reconciliation with God through Jesus Christ. They have not made their peace with God; thus they also have no peace in their life. If they had peace with God, then their anxiety would also disappear, and with their anxiety the struggle for a place in life. One cannot be born again to a living hope through the resurrection of Jesus from the dead if one is not born again through Jesus Christ's act of reconciliation.

On the other hand, many say: How can I believe in the Easter message of the resurrection? I cannot know for certain whether that is true which the Gospels record; I cannot go back and prove it. And if I would simply force myself to believe it because it is recorded in the Bible—assuming that I could so force myself—how would that help me? That would not give me a joyful, living hope. They are entirely right. Such a faith whose authority is merely history has no worth. The real Easter faith does not come from the fact that one believes the report of the apostle without doubting; rather, it comes from the fact that one is reconciled to God through Jesus Christ. This reconciliation is not a mere belief but a rebirth, a new life. Through this reconciliation, godlessness and anxiety are rooted out and one becomes a new man. From this reconciliation through Jesus Christ faith in his resurrection from the dead arises of itself.

Some people have already tried to force themselves to believe in what the Bible reports of the resurrection of Jesus. But it was not so simple. Always doubt interfered; and then one thought that doubt—for example, scientific doubt in the possibility of such a miracle—was the basis of his inability to believe. That goes without saying. Some of the greatest scientists of all times have believed in the resurrection, just as an apostle of early Christianity. Perhaps you also belong to those who would like to believe, who would also like to have this hope of eternal life. But you say you cannot. I wish to tell you precisely why you cannot believe, and I also wish to tell you how you can believe. You cannot believe it because you are not reconciled to God, and you are not reconciled to God because you do not really wish to repent for your godlessness. All unbelief without any exception comes from this unwillingness to obey, from the unwillingness of sin that separates us from God. In the moment when you do that and sincerely acknowledge your sins, then you can also believe in the reconciliation; no, in this moment you are reconciled to God through Jesus Christ and the truth of the Easter message is clear to you. Then you believe in the resurrection, not because it is reported by the apostles but because the resurrected One himself encounters you in a living way as he who unites you with God, as the living Mediator. Now you yourself know it: he lives, he, the Reconciler and Redeemer.

EMIL BRUNNER

ABSOLUTE FAITH AND THE COURAGE TO BE

We have avoided the concept of faith in our description of the courage to be which is based on mystical union with the ground of being as well as in our description of the courage to be which is based on the personal encounter with God. This is partly because the concept of faith has lost its genuine meaning and has received the connotation of "belief in something unbelievable." But this is not the only reason for the use of terms other than faith. The decisive reason is that I do not think either mystical union or personal encounter fulfills the idea of faith. Certainly there is faith in the elevation of the soul above the finite to the infinite, leading to its union with the ground of being. But more than this is included in the concept of faith. And there is faith in the personal encounter with the personal God. But more than this is included in the concept of faith. Faith is the state of being grasped by the power of being-itself. The courage to be is an expression of faith and what "faith" means must be understood through the courage to be. We have defined courage as the self-affirmation of being in spite of non-being. The power of this self-affirmation is the power of being which is effective in every act of courage. Faith is the experience of this power.

PAUL TILLICH

WHAT IS CONTEMPLATION?

CONTEMPLATION is the highest expression of man's intellectual and spiritual life. It is that life itself, fully awake, fully active, fully aware that it is alive. It is spiritual wonder. It is spontaneous awe at the sacredness of life, of being. It is gratitude for life, for awareness and for being. It is a vivid realization of the fact that life and being in us proceed from an invisible, transcendent and infinitely abundant Source. Contemplation is, above all, awareness of the reality of that Source. It *knows* the Source, obscurely, inexplicably, but with a certitude that goes both beyond reason and beyond simple faith. For contemplation is a kind of spiritual vision to which both reason and faith aspire, by their very nature, because without it they must always remain incomplete. Yet contemplation is not vision because it sees "without seeing" and knows "without knowing." It is a more profound depth of faith, a knowledge too deep to be grasped in images, in words or even in clear concepts. It can be suggested by words, by symbols, but in the very moment of trying to indicate what it knows the contemplative mind takes back what it has said, and denies what it has affirmed. For in contemplation we know by "unknowing." Or, better, we know *beyond* all knowing or "unknowing."

Poetry, music and art have something in common with the contemplative experience. But contemplation is beyond aesthetic intuition, beyond art, beyond poetry. Indeed, it is also beyond philosophy, beyond speculative theology. It resumes, transcends and fulfills them all, and yet at the same time it seems in a certain way, to supersede and to deny them all. Contemplation is always beyond our own knowledge, beyond our own light, beyond systems, beyond explanations, beyond discourse, beyond dialogue, beyond our own self. To enter into the realm of contemplation one must in a certain sense die: but this death is in fact the entrance into a higher life. It is a death for the sake of life, which leaves behind all that we can know or treasure as life, as thought, as experience, as joy, as being.

THOMAS MERTON

THE EARTH GROWN LIKE THE MOON: A VISION

The earth
Is like the moon,
Cold crystal,
Flowers of ice.
It is a desert,
Skyless,
Lifeless;
For mankind
Has laid it waste.

The earth is frozen,
Glittering like a jewel,
Yet
Ruined by pride.

Seen from a star,
The earth gleams
Like the moon.
Mount Fuji glistens
And the Alps
Glow in their glory.

Jerusalem,
Tokyo,

The slums of London,
And the underworld
Of Paris—
All are shadows.

Living things
Have left the earth
Forsaken.
They rebel
At dwelling
In its ugliness.
Still the world
Whirls on,
In agony.

Lo, man's sin
Is great
Before his God;
His world
A waste.

Graves of heroes
And of harlots
Both alike
Are dust,
And dust alone.
God has at length
Frozen the world
Cold as the moon.

(And why should not God's love for us
        grow dim,
This world which has no love or use for Him?)

TOYOHIKO KAGAWA

PRAYER

There is only one test of our prayer life really. Are we wanting
God? Do we want Him so much that we'll go on if it takes five,
six, ten years to find Him? With that steady determination not

to let up till we do, a determination that even goes on when there seems no success at all? The primary object of prayer is to know God better; we and our needs should come second.

He did not teach us to pray in long rigmaroles as though the more wordy we are the more sure we are to be heard—we think our self-satisfied judgments are His. Spiritual silence is turning our soul, in quietness, to Him — a power beyond ourselves. You know what a tangle our minds get into, how difficult it seems to disentangle the Voice of God. You have to let Him do that, and to learn to keep one's ear tuned is a very great adventure. 'In returning and rest shall you be saved.'

Until we know Him as 'Thou' and the 'Thou' the supreme importance to us, what can we witness?

There can be all the difference in the world between beginning a prayer with 'O Almighty God' and beginning it with 'Thou' breathed to Someone—*there*. We need to practice that, until the Presence becomes so real that He is in deed and truth possessing the very centre where for us the important 'I' stands so supreme.

FLORENCE ALLSHORN

NOT FOR THE WISE

I am afraid that prayer is really not for the wise. The wise avoid it on two bases, at least two. In the first place, if there really is a God who has this power to heal, to make whole, then it is wise to be very cautious indeed because if you go to him for healing, healing may be exactly what you will receive, and are you entirely sure that you want to be healed? By all accounts, after all, the process is not necessarily either quick or easy. And in the meanwhile, things could be a great deal worse. "Lord, take my sin from me—but not yet," Saint Augustine is said to have prayed. It is a wise man who bewares of God bearing gifts. In the second place, the wise look at twentieth-century man—civilized, rational, and at great cost emancipated from the dark superstitions of the past—and suggest that to petition some unseen power for special favors is a very childish procedure indeed. . . .

In honesty you have to admit to a wise man that prayer is not for the wise, not for the prudent, not for the sophisticated. Instead it is for those who recognize that in face of their deepest needs, all their wisdom is quite helpless. It is for those who are willing to persist in doing something that is both childish and crucial.

FREDERICK BUECHNER

CHANGE COMES THROUGH PERSONS

Whether one speaks of the tradition of John or of Luke, a single impression abides. Human change invariably occurs through the agency of persons. Other species of change, worked by influences more or less impersonal (our century has multiplied these forms to an almost unbearable degree), are invariably frivolous or destructive. The point is worth dwelling on, not only because talk of change and analysis of change are so much in the air today. More nearly to our point is the fact that personal change, and the kind of social change that loses none of its personalism, is a law of life itself . . . .

The change to which Christ invites us is in fact a recovery of, or a strengthening of, the sense of the person. New directions often have their finest value precisely in this. Underlying the sense of unrest with old ways of thought, with outworn language, predictable reactions, climates of life that are imported or stale or false, is something extremely precious. The person is coming through once more. He may have felt himself duped or trapped; he may have sensed that a given atmosphere was forbidding him to be himself. Or he could not accept the terms under which life was presented; they seemed to him arbitrary or childish or sterile. And if he is fortunate, he breaks through; and in breaking through, not with desperation or clumsy or wounding acts, but with the quiet determination of the Spirit, he finds that communion is possible with others too. Those others, perhaps engaged in the same ideal and pursuing the same form of life, had seemed to form a ring of silence around him. And how strange it is, he thinks, that silence should have prevailed so long, that mere politeness and a sense of amenities should have prevented each from touching the heart and hope of the other.

The greatest changes within human life thus come to pass when a man has awakened to the existence of his brethren. And when we come to think of our own times, we must take heart that such an awakening is actually occuring all around us, in the most unexpected places and in lives one would have placed least hope in. What a momentous thing it is that Christians who are willing to spend themselves for their brethren need never stand alone. There are always others ready to stand with us; altruism cuts across all lines of dogma and culture, allowing a brother to meet a brother's hand across the human need one is determined to serve.

DANIEL BERRIGAN

I STILL BELIEVE

I have the audacity to believe that peoples everywhere can have three meals a day for their tired bodies, education and culture for their minds, and dignity, equality and freedom for their spirits. I believe that what self-centered men have torn down, men other-centered can build up. I still believe that one day mankind will bow before the altars of God and be crowned triumphant over war and bloodshed, and non-violent redemptive goodwill will proclaim the rule of the land. "And the lion and the lamb shall lie down together and every man shall sit under his own vine and fig tree and none shall be afraid." I still believe that we shall overcome.

MARTIN LUTHER KING, JR.

PRAY FOR YOUR OWN DISCOVERY

There exists some point at which I can meet God in a real and experimental contact with His infinite actuality. This is the "place" of God, His sanctuary—it is the point where my contingent being depends upon His love. Within myself is a meta-phorical apex of existence at which I am held in being by my Creator.

God utters me like a word containing a partial thought of Himself.

A word will never be able to comprehend the voice that utters it.

But if I am true to the concept that God utters in me, if I am true to the thought of Him I was meant to embody, I shall be full of His actuality and find Him everywhere in myself, and find myself nowhere. I shall be lost in Him: that is, I shall find myself. I shall be "saved."

It is a pity that the beautiful Christian metaphor "salva-tion" has come to be so hackneyed and therefore so despised. It has been turned into a vapid synonym for "piety"—not even a truly ethical concept. "Salvation" is something far beyond ethical propriety. The word connotes a deep respect for the fundamental metaphysical reality of man. It reflects God's own infinite concern for man, God's love and care for man's inmost being, God's love for all that is His own in man, His son. It is not only human nature that is "saved" by the divine mercy, but above all the human *person*. The object of salva-tion is that which is unique, irreplaceable, incommunicable— that which is myself alone. This true inner self must be drawn up like a jewel from the bottom of the sea, rescued from con-fusion, from indistinction, from immersion in the common, the nondescript, the trivial, the sordid, the evanescent.

THOMAS MERTON

TO KNOW HE IS WITH YOU

Now faith is not an easy thing to come by. You are fortunate if you have been ill enough to think that only faith will save you. Then you have to have it. You have to have it when your body is saying the opposite—that it is in the thrall, not of 'more abundant life', but of sick life. You can gull yourself about the soul, not the body. You have to reiterate to yourself, pulling your imagination up all the time, the fact that God is with life, that sickness is the enemy, that God is stronger than the enemy, and He has looked on you, His creation, and said: 'It is very good'. You have to know that He is with you in your faith, redeeming your sickness, and that it is His will that you have a perfect body as He made it to be. You may fail and fail but you may not go back on that faith.

It is the same with the soul, that part of you that is your intrinsic being, not your thoughts only, but you as you are, very you. It is sick with pride, lethargy, self-righteousness, whatever it is, and you go under again and again; you cannot love, it doesn't seem to be in you to love with anything like the touchiness with which you resent, the coldness you feel unless someone touches your emotions and makes it easy for you to respond. That is your soul sickness and that is where, just as in the body, you have to regrip your faith again and again. Despondency, depression, self-pity, like sickness these were the things Jesus fought against unto death; these were the devils against Him all the time. He refused to believe they were His children. They were not His children, they were Satan possessing and endeavouring to destroy His children. 'Get thee behind me, Satan', He says to Peter, not 'Get thee behind me, Peter', as we do. We say: 'She is jealous', not 'Jealousy possesses her'.

FLORENCE ALLSHORN

THE NEW BEING

In his letter, Paul combines New Creation with reconciliation. The message of reconciliation is: Be reconciled to God. Cease to be hostile to Him, for He is never hostile to you. The message of reconciliation is not that God needs to be reconciled. How could He be? Since He is the source and power of reconciliation, who could reconcile Him? Pagans and Jews and Christians—all of us have tried and are trying to reconcile Him by rites and sacraments, by prayers and services, by moral behavior and works of charity. But if we try this, if we try to give something to Him, to show good deeds which may appease Him, we fail. It is never enough; we never can satisfy

Him because there is an infinite demand upon us. And since we cannot appease Him, we grow hostile toward Him. Have you ever noticed how much hostility against God dwells in the depths of the good and honest people, in those who excel in works of charity, in piety and religious zeal? This cannot be otherwise; for one is hostile, consciously or unconsciously, toward those by whom one feels rejected. Everybody is in this predicament, whether he calls that which rejects him "God," or "nature," or "destiny," or "social conditions." Everybody carries a hostility toward the existence into which he has been thrown, toward the hidden powers which determine his life and that of the universe, toward that which makes him guilty and that threatens him with destruction because he has become guilty. We all feel rejected and hostile toward what has rejected us. We all try to appease it and in failing, we become more hostile. This happens often unnoticed by ourselves. But there are two symptoms which we hardly can avoid noticing: The hostility against ourselves and the hostility against others. One speaks so often of pride and arrogance and self-certainty and complacency in people. But this is, in most cases, the superficial level of their being. Below this, in a deeper level, there is self-rejection, disgust, and even hatred of one's self. Be reconciled to God; that means at the same time, be reconciled to ourselves. But we are not; we try to appease ourselves. We try to make ourselves more acceptable to our own judgment and, when we fail, we grow more hostile toward ourselves. And he who feels rejected by God and who rejects himself feels also rejected by the others. As he grows hostile toward destiny, and hostile toward himself, he also grows hostile toward other men. If we are often horrified by the unconscious or conscious hostility people betray toward us or about our own hostility toward people whom we believe we love, let us not forget: They feel rejected by us; we feel rejected by them. They tried hard to make themselves acceptable to us, and they failed. We tried hard to make ourselves acceptable to them and we failed. And their and our hositilty grew. Be reconciled with God—that means, at the same time, be reconciled with the others! But it does not mean try to reconcile the others, as it does not mean try to reconcile yourselves. Try to reconcile God. You will fail. This is the message:

A new reality has appeared in which you are reconciled. To enter the New Being we do not need to show anything. We must only be open to be grasped by it, although we have nothing to show.

Being reconciled—that is the first mark of the New Reality. And being reunited is its second mark. Reconciliation makes reunion possible. The New Creation is the reality in which the separated is reunited. The New Being is manifest in the Christ because in Him the separation never overcame the unity between Him and God, between Him and mankind, between Him and Himself. This gives His picture in the Gospels its overwhelming and inexhaustible power. In Him we look at a human life that maintained the union in spite of everything that drove Him into separation. He represents and mediates the power of the New Being because He represents and mediates the power of an undisrupted union. Where the New Reality appears, one feels united with God, the ground and meaning of one's existence. One has what has been called the love of one's destiny, and what, today, we might call the courage to take upon ourselves our own anxiety. Then one has the astonishing experience of feeling reunited with one's self, not in pride and false self-satisfaction, but in a deep self-acceptance. One accepts one's self as something which is eternally important, eternally loved, eternally accepted. The disgust at one's self, the hatred of one's self has disappeared. There is a center, a direction, a meaning for life. All healing—bodily and mental—creates this reunion of one's self with one's self. Where there is real healing, there is the New Being, the New Creation. But real healing is not where only a part of body or mind is reunited with the whole, but where the whole itself, our whole being, our whole personality is united with itself. The New Creation is healing creation because it creates reunion with oneself. And it creates reunion with the others. Nothing is more distinctive of the Old Being than the separation of man from man. Nothing is more passionately demanded than social healing, than the New Being within history and human relationships. Religion and Christianity are under strong accusation that they have not brought reunion into human history. Who could deny the truth of this challenge. Nevertheless, mankind still lives; and it could not live any more if the power of separation had not been permanently conquered by the power of reunion, of healing, of the New Creation. Where one is grasped by a human face as human, although one has to overcome personal distaste, or racial strangeness, or national conflicts, or the differences of sex, of age, of beauty, of strength, of knowledge, and all the other innumerable causes of separation — *there* New Creation happens! Mankind lives because this happens again and again. And if the Church which is the assembly of God has an ultimate significance, this is its significance: That here the reunion of man to man is pronounced and confessed and realized, even if in fragments and weaknesses and distortions.

Reconciliation, reunion, resurrection—this is the New Creation, the New Being, the new state of things. Do we participate in it? The message of Christianity is not Christianity, but a New Reality. A new state of things has appeared, it still appears; it is hidden and visible, it is there and it is here. Accept it, enter into it. Let it grasp you.

PAUL TILLICH

COSTLY GRACE

Yet the outcome of the Reformation was the victory, not of Luther's perception of grace in all its purity and costliness, but of the vigilant religious instinct of man for the place where grace is to be obtained at the cheapest price. All that was needed was a subtle and almost imperceptible change of emphasis, and the damage was done. Luther had taught that man cannot stand before God, however religious his works and ways may be, because at bottom he is always seeking his own interests. In the depth of his misery, Luther had grasped by faith the free and unconditional forgiveness of all his sins. That experience taught him that this grace had cost him his very life, and must continue to cost him the same price day by day. So far from dispensing him from discipleship, this grace only made him a more earnest disciple. When he spoke of grace, Luther always implied as a corollary that it cost him his own life, the life which was now for the first time subjected to the absolute obedience of Christ. Only so could he speak of grace. Luther had said that grace alone can save; his followers took up his doctrine and repeated it word for word. But they left out its invariable corollary, the obligation of discipleship. There was no need for Luther always to mention that corollary explicitly for he always spoke as one who had been led by grace to the strictest following of Christ. Judged by the standard of Luther's doctrine, that of his followers was unassailable, and yet their orthodoxy spelt the end and destruction of the Reformation as the revelation on earth of the costly grace of God. The justification of the sinner in the world degenerated into the justification of sin and the world. Costly grace was turned into cheap grace without discipleship. . . .

This cheap grace has been no less disastrous to our own spiritual lives. Instead of opening up the way to Christ it has closed it. Instead of calling us to follow Christ, it has hardened us in our disobedience. Perhaps we had once heard the gracious call to follow him, and had at this command even taken the first four steps along the path of discipleship in the discipline of obedience only to find ourselves confronted by the word of cheap grace. Was that not merciless and hard? The only effect that such a word could have on us was to bar our way to progress, and seduce to the mediocre level of the world, quenching the joy of discipleship by telling us that we were spending our strength and disciplining ourselves in vain — all of which was not merely useless, but extremely dangerous. After all, we were told, our salvation has already been accomplished by the grace of God. The smoking flax was mercilessly extinguished. It was unkind to speak to men like this, for such a cheap offer could only leave them bewildered and tempt them from the way to which they had been called by Christ. Having laid hold on cheap grace, they were barred for ever from the knowledge of costly grace. Deceived and weakened, men felt that they were strong now that they were in possession of this cheap grace — whereas they had in fact lost the power to live the life of discipleship and obedience. The word of cheap grace has been the ruin of more Christians than any commandment of works.

. . . To put it quite simply, we must undertake this task because we are now ready to admit that we no longer stand in the path of true discipleship. We confess that, although our Church is orthodox as far as her doctrine of grace is concerned we are no longer sure that we are members of a Church which follows its Lord. We must therefore attempt to recover a true understanding of the mutual relation between grace and discipleship. The issue can no longer be evaded. It is becoming clearer every day that the most urgent problem besetting our Church is this: How can we live the Christian life in the modern world?

Happy are they who have reached the end of the road we seek to tread, who are astonished to discover the by no means self-evident truth that grace is costly just because it is the grace of God in Jesus Christ. Happy are the simple followers of Jesus Christ who have been overcome by his grace, and are able to sing the praises of the all-sufficient grace of Christ with humbleness of heart. Happy are they who, knowing that grace, can live in the world without being of it, who, by following Jesus Christ, are so assured of their heavenly citizenship that they are truly free to live their lives in this world. Happy are they who know that discipleship simply means the life which springs from grace, and that grace simply means discipleship. Happy are they who have become Christians in this sense of the word. For them the word of grace has proved a fount of mercy.

DIETRICH BONHOEFFER

A HEART OF FAITH

Thou who art over us,
Thou who art one of us,
Thou who *art*—
Also within us,
May all see Thee—in me also,
May I prepare the way for Thee,
May I thank Thee for all that shall fall to my lot,
May I also not forget the needs of others.
Keep me in Thy love
As Thou wouldest that all should be kept in mine.

May everything in this my being be directed to Thy glory
And may I never despair.
For I am under Thy hand,
And in Thee is all power and goodness.

Give me a pure heart—that I may see Thee,
A humble heart—that I may hear Thee,
A heart of love—that I may serve Thee,
A heart of faith—that I may abide in Thee.

DAG HAMMARSKJÖLD

WHO ARE WE, ANYWAY?

'By grace *you* have been saved!' How strange to have this message addressed to us! Who are we, anyway? Let me tell you quite frankly: we are all together great sinners. Please understand me: I include myself. I stand ready to confess being the greatest sinner among you all; yet you may then not exclude yourself from the group! Sinners are people who in the judgment of God, and perhaps of their own consciences, missed and lost their way, who are not just a little, but totally guilty, hopelessly indebted and lost not only in time, but in eternity. We are such sinners. And we are prisoners. Believe me, there is a captivity much worse than the captivity in this house. There are walls much thicker and doors much heavier than those closed upon you. All of us, the people without and you within, are prisoners of our own obstinacy, of our many greeds, of our various anxieties, of our mistrust and in the last analysis of our unbelief. We are all sufferers. Most of all we suffer from ourselves. We each make life difficult for ourselves and in so doing for our fellowmen. We suffer from life's lack of meaning. We suffer in the shadow of death and of eternal judgment toward which we are moving. We spend our life in the midst of a whole world of sin and captivity and suffering . . .

Because we are saved by no other than Jesus Christ, we are saved *by grace*. This means that we did not deserve to be saved. What we deserved would be quite different. We cannot secure salvation for ourselves. Did you read in the newspapers the other day that man will soon be able to produce an artificial moon? But we cannot produce our salvation. No one can be proud of being saved. Each one can only fold his hands in great lowliness of heart and be thankful like a child. Consequently we shall never possess salvation as our property. We may only receive it as a gift over and over again, with hands outstretched. *'By grace* you have been saved!' This means constantly to look away from ourselves to God and to the man on the cross where this truth is revealed. This truth is ever anew to be believed and to be grasped by faith. To believe means to look to Jesus Christ and to God and to trust that there is the truth for us, for our lives, for the life of all men.

KARL BARTH

WHOEVER WE ARE

At its heart most theology, like most fiction, is essentially autobiography. Aquinas, Calvin, Barth, Tillich, working out their systems in their own ways and in their own language, are all telling us the stories of their lives, and if you press them far enough, even at their most cerebral and forbidding, you find an experience of flesh and blood, a human face smiling or frowning or weeping or covering its eyes before something that happened once. What happened once may be no more than a child falling sick, a thunderstorm, a dream, and yet it made for the face and inside the face a difference which no theology can ever entirely convey or entirely conceal.

But for the theologian, it would seem, what happened once, the experience of flesh and blood that may lie at the root of the idea, never appears substantial enough to verify the idea, or at least by his nature the theologian chooses to set forth the idea in another language and to argue for its validity on another basis, and thus between the idea and the experience a great deal intervenes. But there is another class of men—at their best they are poets, at their worst artful dodgers—for whom the idea and the experience, the idea and the image, remain inseparable, and it is somewhere in this class that I belong. That is to say, I cannot talk about God or sin or grace, for example, without at the same time talking about those parts of my own experience where these ideas became compelling and real.

. . . The occasional, obscure glimmering through of grace. The muffled presence of the holy. The images always broken, partial, ambiguous, of Christ. If a vision of Christ, then a vision such as those two stragglers had at Emmaus at suppertime: just the cracking of crust as the loaf came apart in his hands ragged and white before in those most poignant words of all scripture, "He vanished from their sight"—whoever he was, whoever they were. Whoever we are.

FREDERICK BUECHNER

WHO PUT THE QUESTION?

Whitsuntide, 1961

I don't know Who—or what—put the question, I don't know when it was put. I don't even remember answering. But at some moment I did answer *Yes* to Someone—or Something— and from that hour I was certain that existence is meaningful and that, therefore, my life, in self-surrender, had a goal.

From that moment I have known what it means "not to look back," and "to take no thought for the morrow."

Led by the Ariadne's thread of my answer through the labyrinth of Life, I came to a time and place where I realized that the Way leads to a triumph which is a catastrophe, and to a catastrophe which is a triumph, that the price for committing one's life would be reproach, and that the only elevation possible to man lies in the depths of humiliation. After that, the word "courage" lost its meaning, since nothing could be taken from me.

As I continued along the Way, I learned, step by step, word by word, that behind every saying in the Gospels stands one man and one man's experience. Also behind the prayer that the cup might pass from him and his promise to drink it. Also behind each of the words from the Cross.

DAG HAMMARSKJÖLD

48

WHO AM I?

Who am I? They often tell me
I step from my cell's confinement
calmly, cheerfully, firmly,
like a squire from his country-house.
Who am I? They often tell me
I talk to my warders
freely and friendly and clearly,
as though it were mine to command.
Who am I? They also tell me
I bear the days of misfortune
equably, smilingly, proudly,
like one accustomed to win.

Am I then really all that which other men tell of?
Or am I only what I know of myself,
restless and longing and sick, like a bird in a cage,
struggling for breath, as though hands were compressing
    my throat,
yearning for colours, for flowers, for the voices of birds,
thirsting for words of kindness, for neighbourliness,
tossing in expectation of great events,
powerlessly trembling for friends at an infinite distance,
weary and empty at praying, at thinking, at making,
faint, and ready to say farewell to it all?
Who am I? This or the other?
Am I one person today, and tomorrow another?
and before myself a contemptibly woebegone weakling?
Or is something within me still like a beaten army,
fleeing in disorder from victory already achieved?

Who am I? They mock me, these lonely questions of mine.
Whoever I am, thou knowest, O God, I am thine.

DIETRICH BONHOEFFER

WHO HE IS

He comes to us as One unknown, without a name, as of old, by the lake-side, He came to those men who knew Him not. He speaks to us the same word: "Follow thou me!" and sets us to the tasks which He has to fulfil for our time. He commands. And to those who obey Him, whether they be wise or simple, He will reveal Himself in the toils, the conflicts, the sufferings which they shall pass through in His fellowship, and, as an ineffable mystery, they shall learn in their own experience Who He is.

ALBERT SCHWEITZER

WITNESS

2

WITNESS

WITNESS

In the section "Faith, Hope, and Love," we have already met many of these witnesses. New to our company is a martyr of the Nazi days, Paul Schneider, a pastor who came into conflict with officials when he denounced the pagan political mythology that Nazism was superimposing on the Christian concept of eternity. Arrested and released, he continued to preach from the pulpit from which he was barred. He paid for this with his life. His letter is from a book of almost incredible heroism, *Dying We Live*. This story could also easily have gone in the Section entitled "Life and Death," but I have chosen to put more ordinary stories there, if any encounter with death is ordinary. Martin Luther King, Jr., appears here again as do Mother Teresa, Paul Tillich, Roger Schutz, Reinhold Niebuhr, Florence Allshorn and the priests Berrigan and Merton.

Five women appear for the first time. Janet Lacey whose service to the refugees brought her the award, Commander of the British Empire (a startlingly colonial title for this modern woman), Suzanne de Dietrich, the Biblical scholar who has been an intimate friend of the Dutch missionary ecumenist Hendrik Kramer, the first director of the Ecumenical Institute of the World Council of Churches in Bossey, Switzerland, and Willem A. Visser't Hooft, the first general secretary of the World Council of Churches. Suzanne de Dietrich was one of the few women among many famous men of her generation prominent in the activities of the World Student Christian Federation. The enthusiasm and beauty of her Bible studies have been shared with many both through her books, in the Protestant community of Grandchamp and in international encounters at the beautiful rural setting of Bossey, Switzerland.

Dorothy Day is a Roman Catholic convert who grew up in a secular family (her father was a newspaperman) and who sought brotherhood and meaning first in Marxism and other left wing activities of the Twenties. She sought to serve the poor through the *Catholic Worker,* a newspaper she started with the French peasant-philosopher Peter Maurin, and the hospitality houses they ran. Dorothy Day, now in her seventies, continues to pursue peace (pacifist in the last war before it was even remotely commonplace) and justice for the poor. Like Mother Teresa her interest is not in parties or structures but in humble, loving service to the outcast. Her stints in prisons for various causes have also made her desperately interested in the conditions in prisons and their failure to rehabilitate. Simone Weil, the French philosopher of Jewish birth, died during her exile from France in World War II. Monica Furlong is a British journalist who writes television criticism and has in recent years written two small books with large publics, *With Love to the Church* and *Contemplation.*

D. T. Niles, the evangelist and preacher from Ceylon with a burning passion for witness and unity, is another of the recently dead who are apt to be forgotten too quickly. This luminous man who spoke so eloquently to audiences in America and Europe was one of the great Asian missionaries to the West. There will probably be more and more of these witnesses coming from Latin America, Asia, and Africa, bringing the Gospel back to the lands where the message and zeal have grown cold.

Clarence Jordan, a Georgia farmer and Baptist minister, had a belief in the equality of all men which brought him into sharp conflict with his white neighbors in Georgia. His community Koinonia still exists as a cooperative farm and Christian community whose pecans and other products are sold across the nation and whose Cotton Patch Gospel message is still going strong. The passages from Jordan are his own freely idiomatic translations from Greek and Hebrew and come from his *Cotton Patch Sermons.*

Dom Helder Câmara, the archbishop of Olinda and Recife in northeast Brazil, was nominated for the Nobel Peace Prize because of his outspoken identification with the poor and the oppressed. Small in stature, he is large in compassion and understanding.

Michel Quoist, a French priest, is one of the most popular spiritual readers of our times. *Prayers* written in contemporary language is a best seller in French and English.

GO TELL EVERYONE

God's Spirit is in my heart,
He has called me and set me apart,
This is what I have to do,
What I have to do.

He's sent me to give the good news to the poor,
Tell prisoners that they are prisoners no more,
Tell blind people that they can see,
And set the down-trodden free,
And go tell everyone the news that the Kingdom of God
has come,
And go tell everyone the news that God's kingdom has
come.

Just as the Father sent me,
So I'm sending you out to be
My witnesses throughout the world,
The whole of the world.

Don't carry a load in your pack,
You don't need two shirts on your back,
The workman can earn his own keep,
Can earn his own keep.

Don't worry what you have to say,
Don't worry because on that day,
God's Spirit will speak in your heart,
Will speak in your heart.

MOTHER TERESA

SHOW ME IT IS POSSIBLE

It will be useful for us to think for a moment, and find that
place where our little personal strivings towards a more real
Christianity fit in with the world-wide need.

Even if you look at it, as life plays out its drama in our own
town or country village (or in our own inner lives) there are
queer misses that we can't seem to bring together. Most

news, for instance, is bad news, and reading our morning and evening papers, year after year lately, our hearts have been battered and bruised with bad news. I cannot tell, of course, how far the tragedy of the general human fate is your sorrow— most of us recognize ashamedly that our own private cares and troubles and worries absorb us to such an extent that we have little left over to be roused enough to feel any indignant spiritual protest against the suffering of anything so nebulous to us as the human race. Yet in the end it is only that sorrow and protest that can give any dignity and meaning to our lives. We have known of the suffering of bombed-out homes, torn-apart familes driven from their native lands and from one another, people herded like cattle into great huddles of lostness; we read how fearful man is before the threat of the atom bomb and know that he feels no security in the promises of nations; that the post-war world is famine ridden and fear ridden; and perhaps the only thing that we do not know is that all this insecurity of the modern world seeps into the very bones of every child that is born into the world, as it has, whether we recognize it or not, seeped into us.

All that we read and know adds enormously to man's discouragement at this time, and before so much heaped-up depression it is little wonder that a kind of spiritual impotence grips people.

And it is just here that the queer misses come in. The world is faced with bad news, and yet there is a great Christian Church which is reputed to be the custodian of good news; there is the Church's awakened evangelistic concern, and the world's bewildered groping for the light, and yet they seem to pass each other in the dark.

It was just such a bewildered man facing this situation, a young R.A.F. pilot, who said to a Christian, 'Don't try to help me or preach to me, or tell me what I ought to think yet. Don't work for my salvation, show me yours, show me it is possible, and the knowledge that something works will give me courage and belief in mine.'

That is all we are asked to do at the moment, and nothing less will do; and it is much harder to do than was the old type of evangelization. We have to show them where their groping and our finding meet.   FLORENCE ALLSHORN

58

A STYLE OF LIFE

Of course, the difference, the mystery that we call Christian, becomes visible in a style of life, in a formed and illumined conscience. But it is particularly striking today that the outlines of our style of life, when they are very pure and open, coincide more and more with the consciences, the aspirations, and qualities of other lives. The fact can be very disturbing in its first shock. There is a mysterious development of conscience taking place in the world, and this development parallels many new aspects of conscience within the church. It sometimes goes even further, exerting a positive pressure on Christians to take up unpopular causes, to exercise a purer, more courageous presence.

Such reflections lead one to suggest that faith in Christ is attractive to others today not in terms of enclosure and outer world so much as in a mysterious interpenetration of grace that summons a brother to the side of his brother and finds that differences are given a new perspective in mutual service.

Thus the effort toward renewal is not self-centered but relational. The renewal we seek for ourselves is to be found most surely in the strength of the human relationships we are able to create and sustain with others. Our method, our *mystique,* as Péguy called it, is to incarnate relationships, to ground ourselves firmly in other lives, to give visible form to the mystery of Christ's brotherhood and, in the process, to extend the mystery itself, to make it apparent, palatable, attractive.

DANIEL BERRIGAN

THE CHESTNUT TREE

You ask me what I do all day long. Above all I am a student of the word of God, and want to go on being that . . . .

Once again the chestnut tree is preaching a sermon to me. Its bare black branches reach out to me so promisingly the small brown buds for next spring. I can see them close to the window and also in the top branches. They were already there even when the yellow falling foliage was still hiding them. Should we be so thankless and of so little faith that we deliberately overlook among the falling, withered leaves of the church the buds that here too cling tenaciously to trunk and branches?

Dear wife, I believe we know enough out of our own inner experience to speak and to believe for our communities too. ... The Confessional church—it is truly that—is the tree with the buds; the secret congregations within the congregations are the buds of the church. Wherever a pastor is ready to assume a ministry that no longer is a "ministry," that continues to exist even without assurance of state support (because a "position" thus supported would no longer be a religious post), while all calculations and considerations of church politics are at an end, there the spiritual eye sees even now the coming church and its spring. Of course, the world and the faithless churchmen see the bare tree stripped of its cultural and public significance and judge that since the world and the state withhold recognition, it will soon die and serve only for firewood. They take refuge in the tangled vine of the false church and the state religion, rankly overgrowing the truly doomed tree of a godless, self-glorifying and self-complacent world—a vine that will collapse and be burned with the tree of such a transient world.

But we abide in the branches of the poor, bare, despised, and defamed church that reaches its buds out to us with so much promise, and we know that it alone carries the promise that the gates of hell will not prevail against it. In it only can we live in safety, "secure in all our ways"; only in that faith which is the indestructible strength of its life and its burgeoning can true freedom and happiness be found. Let us go on holding only ever more firmly and unequivocally to this faith, live by it and act by it, as the richly "comforted," because this faith alone represents the victory over the prison of this world and its lethal power. "Then let the world with all its vain reward dissolve. Faith perseveres, the Cross will lead us to the crown."

PAUL SCHNEIDER

WAITING FOR GOD

In 1938, I spent ten days at Solesmes, from Palm Sunday to Easter Tuesday, following all the liturgical services. I was suffering from splitting headaches, each sound hurt me like a blow; by an extreme effort of concentration I was able to rise above this wretched flesh, to leave it to suffer by itself, heaped up in a corner, and to find a pure and perfect joy in the unimaginable beauty of the chanting and the words. This experience enabled me by analogy to get a better understanding of the possibility of loving divine love in the midst of affliction. It goes without saying that in the course of these services the thought of the Passion of Christ entered into my being once and for all.

There was a young English Catholic there from whom I gained my first idea of the supernatural power of the sacraments because of the truly angelic radiance with which he seemed to be clothed after going to communion. Chance—for I always prefer saying chance rather than Providence—made of him a messenger to me. For he told me of the existence of those English poets of the seventeenth century who are named metaphysical. In reading them later on, I discovered the poem of which I read you what is unfortunately a very inadequate translation. It is called "Love".* I learned it by heart. Often, at the culminating point of a violent headache, I make myself say it over, concentrating all my attention upon it and clinging with all my soul to the tenderness it enshrines. I used to think I was merely reciting it as a beautiful poem, but without my knowing it the recitation had the virtue of a prayer. It was during one of these recitations that, as I told you, Christ himself came down and took possession of me.

In my arguments about the insolubility of the problem of God I had never foreseen the possibility of that, of a real contact, person to person, here below, between a human being and God. I had vaguely heard tell of things of this kind, but I had never believed in them. In the Fioretti the accounts of apparitions rather put me off if anything, like the miracles in the Gospel. Moreover, in this sudden possession of my Christ, neither my senses nor my imagination had any part; I only

* By George Herbert.

felt in the midst of my suffering the presence of a love, like that which one can read in the smile on a beloved face.

I had never read any mystical works because I had never felt any call to read them. In reading as in other things I have always striven to practice obedience. There is nothing more favorable to intellectual progress, for as far as possible I only read what I am hungry for at the moment when I have an appetite for it, and then I do not read, I eat. God in his mercy had prevented me from reading the mystics, so that it should be evident to me that I had not invented this absolutely unexpected contact.

Yet I still half refused, not my love but my intelligence. For it seemed to me certain, and I still think so today, that one can never wrestle enough with God if one does so out of pure regard for the truth. Christ likes us to prefer truth to him because, before being Christ, he is truth. If one turns aside from him to go toward the truth, one will not go far before falling into his arms.

SIMONE WEIL

CONVERSION

It is a great arrogance to describe one's conversion, but what happened to me was this. In a situation in which I felt a crippling sense of guilt, a sense of total meaninglessness, a sense of growing isolation from those around me, I suffered, to my surprise, a revelation of God. I had never had much sense of God previously. Like most children brought up in this country I had gone occasionally to church, had endured school prayers, never guessing that the ritual incantations about penitence, forgiveness, and love had any more meaning than the jingoistic incantations about patriotism and sacrifice which get cut down to size in the realities of war.

But God was suddenly someone experienced, asserting with tenderness, the beauty and strength of which nearly annihilated me altogether, that I was loved and I was forgiven. It is almost impossible to explain to a non-Christian what this experience consists of, nor why it changes every relationship and every attitude. Abelard came nearest to expressing the heat and the passion of it.

"Set on fire as we are by so great a benefit from the Divine grace, true charity should fear nothing at all. . . . And so our redemption is that supreme love manifested in our case by the passion of Christ, which not only delivers us from the bondage of sin, but also acquires for us the liberty of the sons of God; so that we may fulfil all things from the love rather than from the fear of him, who, as he himself bears witness, showed us grace so great that no greater can be found."

Peter Abelard lived the sort of life which would have brought the Church bad publicity in the Sunday newspapers, and in the wave of puritanism now blowing across the churches it may be too much to expect anyone to appreciate his note of authority. No doubt he would have to endure the blanket condemnation at present thrown over the whole school of "new moralists."

But "set on fire"? Fulfilling "all things from the love rather than from the fear" of God? Where nowadays in the Church do we find that triumphant recognition that the love of God is the grandest of grand passions, or that resolute rejection of guilt is the spur?

But to go back to the process of conversion. As Charles Williams explains in *The Descent of the Dove* the problem for the Christian is time. How is he to make sense of his singular experience in terms of time? What does he do about it, day in and day out?

For those who undergo the shattering experience of conversion there is another problem which often precedes this, which is how to endure the shock of what has happened. In *Beyond all Reason* Morag Coate describes how, unable to find anyone to share her sudden knowledge of God, she drove herself on to ever more esoteric spiritual adventures until she fell over the cliff of schizophrenia. Few people who have undergone a conversion experience will find this hard to understand. Romantic love, if it goes wrong, brings the most stable people near to psychosis. Religious passion uncovers the great agonies of acceptance and rejection at a still deeper level, healing or wounding the personality at its center. In a foreword to Miss Coate's book, the psychiatrist R. D. Laing suggests that one of the author's greatest misfortunes was that, at the time when she most needed to share her shattering experience of God, she did not "find her guru." I was luckier in that I knew a priest who had both acted as a kind of catalyst of truth in my first critical examination of religion before my conversion, and who was able to bear the first shock of it with me afterwards. I owe him an immense debt, and I hope he will not interpret anything I have written as an attack upon him or upon his explanation of Christian doctrines and ideas which at the time meant so much to me.

But the Church has to exist in time; I had to be a Christian in time, and the disillusion cut deep. Not the disillusion of finding that the certainty of conversion did not last. After fourteen years the awareness of love and forgiveness remains as strong as if it had happened an hour ago. Not the disillusion of discovering how hard it is to love, or how terrifying evil can be if you challenge it directly.

The disillusion I am talking about is the disillusion of discovering that the Church can behave like anti-Christ, that Christians can use their faith as a protection against ever seeing the truth or against exposing themselves to life and experience in any genuine way at all.

MONICA FURLONG

THE POWER OF LOVE

After two thousand years are we still able to realize what it means to say, "God is Love"? The writer of the First Epistle of John certainly knew what he wrote, for he drew the consequences: "He who abides in love abides in God, and God abides in him." God's abiding in us, making us His dwelling place, is the same thing as our abiding in love, as our having love as the sphere of our habitation. God and love are not two realities; they are one. God's Being is the being of love and God's infinite power of Being is the infinite power of love. Therefore, he who professes devotion to God may abide in God if he abides in love, or he may not abide in God if he does not abide in love. And he who does not speak of God may abide in love. And he who does not speak of God may abide in Him if he is abiding in love. And since the manifestation of God as love is His manifestation in Jesus the Christ, Jesus can say that many of those who do not know Him, belong to Him, and that many of those who confess their allegiance to Him do not belong to Him. The criterion, the only ultimate criterion, is love. For God is love and the divine love is triumphantly manifest in Christ the Crucified.

Let me tell you the story of a woman who died a few years ago and whose life was spent abiding in love, although she rarely, if ever, used the name of God, and though she would have been surprised had someone told her that she belonged to Him who judges all men, because He is love and love is the only criterion of His judgment.

Her name was Elsa Brandstrom, the daughter of a former Swedish ambassador to Russia. But her name in the mouths and hearts of hundreds of thousands of prisoners of war during the First World War was the Angel of Siberia. She was an irrefutable, living witness to the truth that love is the ultimate power of Being, even in a century which belongs to the darkest, most destructive and cruel of all centuries since the dawn of mankind.

At the beginning of the First World War, when Elsa Brandstrom was twenty-four years old, she looked out of the window of the Swedish Embassy in what was then St. Petersburg and saw the German prisoners of war being driven through the streets on their way to Siberia. From that moment on she could no longer endure the splendor of the diplomatic life of which, up to then, she had been a beautiful and vigorous center. She became a nurse and began visiting the prison camps. There she saw unspeakable horrors and she, a girl of twenty-four, began, almost alone, the fight of love against cruelty, and she prevailed. She had to fight against the resistance and suspicion of the authorities and she prevailed. She had to fight against the brutality and lawlessness of the prison guards and she prevailed. She had to fight against cold, hunger, dirt and illness, against the conditions of an undeveloped country and destructive war, and she prevailed. Love gave her wisdom with innocence, and daring with foresight. And whenever she appeared despair was conquered and sorrow healed. She visited the hungry and gave them food. She saw the thirsty and gave them to drink. She welcomed the strangers, clothed the naked and strengthened the sick. She herself fell ill and was imprisoned, but God was abiding in her. The irresistible power of love was with her.

And she never ceased to be driven by this power. After the war she initiated a great work for the orphans of German and Russian prisoners of war. The sight of her among these children whose sole ever-shining sun she was, must have been a decisive religious impression for many people. With the coming of the Nazis, she and her husband were forced to leave Germany and come to this country. Here she became the helper of innumerable European refugees, and for ten years I was able personally to observe the creative genius of her love. We never had a theological conversation. It was unnecessary. She made God transparent in every moment. For God, who is love, was abiding in her and she in Him. She aroused the love of millions towards herself and towards that for which she was transparent—the God who is love. On her deathbed she received a delegate from the king and people of Sweden, representing innumerable people all over Europe, assuring her that she would never be forgotten by those to whom she had given back the meaning of their lives.

It is a rare gift to meet a human being in whom love—and this means God—is so overwhelmingly manifest. It undercuts theological arrogance as well as pious isolation. It is more than justice and it is greater than faith and hope. It is the presence of God Himself. For God is love. And in every moment of genuine love we are dwelling in God and God in us.

PAUL TILLICH

RELEASE OTHERS

Jesus is not content to bring those who believe in him into the joyful liberty of the children of God: he wants them in their turn to go out and release others, for by the power of the Spirit the word which they have received, and which has set them free, will become an overflowing fountain of strength and light for those who will listen to them.[1]

To believe in him is to pass from darkness to light, from death to life, from bondage to liberty.

SUZANNE de DIETRICH

[1] I John 7:37-38.

FATHER AND MOTHER

"We now stand under a new law"—that is the first certainty. What God demands of me is faith, the willingness to trust myself in his hands and to leave myself there even when I do not trust him. What does that mean? When we study the book of Psalms, again and again we find the psalmist in a mood of quarreling with God, finding fault with God, arguing with God. The psalmist seems to take liberties with God which we do not take. It is a good thing to be able to do that. If you cannot scold God when life goes wrong, whom else can you scold?

I sometimes like to put it to myself like this. We must learn to know God not only as father but also as mother. When things go wrong in the house, maybe we do not like to grumble against father, but we would like to grumble against mother. There is a sense in which there is a closeness between mother and child which does not exist between father and child. And the psalmist seems to know how to treat God as mother—to go to God and say: "You had no business to do this." "Why did you do this?" "I am angry because you did this." But it is to God that the psalmist goes and to whom he speaks. Faith is to trust oneself in God's hands even when one has lost faith—to leave oneself there, to be in mother's arms. The child yells if it wants to yell, but still it is in its mother's arms. That is the situation which Paul says has been created for us in the gospel; and this is made effectual by the Holy Spirit which teaches us to say, "My Father."

.   .   .   .   .   .

The truth that God is Father is what you will not find in any other religion except Christianity. No wonder Paul says, "Nobody has ever learned to call God Father except in and through the Holy Spirit." The Holy Spirit teaches me to call God Father, to believe that God thinks of me as me. And then Paul goes on: In order to come to this experience I don't have to be a particular kind of person, because this is for all creation. At the end of the eleventh chapter, where this discussion ends, Paul closes with those glorious words: "For of him, and through him, and to him, are all things." All things and, therefore, I also. Or, to use the words of Charles Wesley, "So wide it passed by none, or it had passed by me." The mercy of God is so wide, the grace of God is so wide, that it did not pass anyone by. That is why I know that it did not pass me by. I was the last on the list.

D.T. NILES

PEACEMAKING IS HARD

"Peacemaking is hard, hard almost as war." It seems to us that, when we understand how hard war is, we understand the obligation to make peace. There will be no moral equivalent of war until we engage the price of war—technological terror, scorched earth, millions of dead Indochinese, young American lives snuffed out, a ruined society in Southeast Asia, untold billions of treasure wasted—sorrow, despair, desperation, rage. If we understand modern war, we understand the effort that peace requires. And we settle for nothing but total peace.

We choose peace, not in rhetoric alone, but in truth, love, in risk, suffering, in every element of our lives. Even if that meant loss of possession, public disgrace, prison, death. To lose that others might gain, to be imprisoned that others might be free, to die that others might live, this is the stuff of life, this is humanity in its fullest glory.

The Master so spoke, following the great Jewish prophets: "This is my commandment, love one another as I have loved you. There is no greater love than this, that a man should lay down his life for his friends. You are my friends, if you do what I command you." (John 15:13-14).

DANIEL BERRIGAN

CREATIVE EXTREMISTS

Oppressed people cannot remain oppressed forever. The yearning for freedom eventually manifests itself, and that is what has happened to the American Negro. Something within has reminded him of his birthright of freedom and something without has reminded him that it can be gained. Consciously or unconsciously, he has been caught up by the *zeitgeist,* and with his black brothers of Africa and his brown and yellow brothers of Asia, South America and the Caribbean, the United States Negro is moving with a sense of great urgency toward the promised land of racial justice. If one recognizes this vital urge that has engulfed the Negro community, one should readily understand why public demonstrations are taking place. The Negro has many pent-up resentments and latent frustrations, and he must release them. So let him march; let him make prayer pilgrimages to the city hall; let him go on freedom rides—and try to understand why he must do so. If his repressed emotions are not released in nonviolent ways, they will seek expression through violence; this is not a threat but a fact of history. So I have not said to my people: "Get rid of your discontent." Rather, I have tried to say that this normal and healthy discontent can be channeled into the creative outlet of nonviolent direct action. And now this approach is being termed extremist.

But though I was initially disappointed at being categorized as an extremist, as I continued to think about the matter I gradually gained a measure of satisfaction from the label. Was not Jesus an extremist for love: "Love your enemies, bless them that curse you, do good to them that hate you, and pray for them which despitefully use you, and persecute you." Was not Amos an extremist for justice: "Let justice roll down like waters and righteousness like an everflowing stream." Was not Paul an extremist for the Christian gospel: "I bear in my body the marks of the Lord Jesus." Was not Martin Luther an extremist: "Here I stand, I cannot do otherwise, so help me God." And John Bunyan: "I will stay in jail to the end of my days before I make a butchery of my conscience." And Abraham Lincoln: "This nation cannot survive half slave and half free." And Thomas Jefferson: "We hold these truths to be self-evident, that all men are created equal ..." So the question is not whether we will be extremists, but what kind of extremists we will be. Will we be extremists for hate or for love? Will we be extremists for the preservation of injustice or for the extension of justice? In that dramatic scene on Calvary's hill three men were crucified. We must never forget that all three were crucified for the same crime—the crime of extremism. Two were extremists for immorality, and thus fell below their environment. The other, Jesus Christ, was an extremist for love, truth and goodness, and thereby rose above his environment. Perhaps the South, the nation and the world are in dire need of creative extremists.

MARTIN LUTHER KING, JR.

ON HEARING THE TRUTH

A nation is very sick, a government is very weak, when neither the one nor the other can bear to be told the truth. A heavy silence falls because 'the times are bad.' Thus Amos still says to us young men and women are still dying of thirst. Still people have a hunger and thirst to 'hear the words of the Lord'[1] but they wander all over the world and do not find it.

[1] Amos 8:11-14.

SUZANNE de DIETRICH

DAILY PRAYER:* JESUS MY PATIENT

Dearest Lord, may I see you today and every day in the person of your sick, and, whilst nursing them, minister unto you. Though you hide yourself behind the unattractive disguise of the irritable, the exacting, the unreasonable, may I still recognize you, and say:

'Jesus, my patient, how sweet it is to serve you.' Lord, give me this seeing faith, then my work will never be monotonous.

* For the Children's Home.

I will ever find joy in humouring the fancies and gratifying the wishes of all poor sufferers.

O beloved sick, how doubly dear you are to me, when you personify Christ; and what a privilege is mine to be allowed to tend you.

Sweetest Lord, make me appreciative of the dignity of my high vocation, and its many responsibilities. Never permit me to disgrace it by giving way to coldness, unkindness, or impatience.

And O God, while you are Jesus, my patient, deign also to be to me a patient Jesus, bearing with my faults, looking only to my intention, which is to love and serve you in the person of each of your sick.

Lord, increase my faith, bless my efforts and work, now and for evermore. Amen.

MOTHER TERESA

FIRST ENLIST

Apart from Jesus, men argue whether God is love; in his presence men believe it and live by it. Apart from Jesus, men argue about the meaning of life; in his presence they cease arguing and begin to follow. Apart from Jesus, men argue about human responsibility for sin; in his presence they fall down and ask forgiveness. To meet him is to know the truth, the truth that sets men free.

But Jesus is significant not only for truth but also for life. All life's questions find their solution in him. He is life's Lord. To live with him is to live powerfully, to live in him is to live abundantly. For very life's sake we dare not refuse to meet him, for he is life. But Jesus is more even than that: he is the way. And to us that more is significant, for we are concerned not only with abundant life hereafter, but also with abundant life here. We are concerned with schemes of practical re-form to make this our present world a better world to live in. For many the claim of Christ that he is the way is the most compelling claim of all. But is he?

71

Has he a vision of that better world? Yes, he has, and no man has ever conceived a grander ideal than his of the Kingdom of God operative on earth. Has he a method and technique? He has, a method without compulsion of casuistry, the only method which up to date has achieved anything of lasting value. Has he a plan? Yes, he has: first Galilee, then Jerusalem, then Gethsemane and Calvary, and finally Easter Morning.

But what about actual plans for us, the hard details of this campaign to make a better world? Christ's answer to that is simply *"first enlist."* Does that seem to be an evading of the issue? Nevertheless it is his answer. First enlist, and then you will receive orders. First befriend Me and then you will know My purpose. First follow Me and then you will learn My plans. But Master Christ! How do I know that Thy way leads to that better world? You know because it is My way.

To me that answer is sufficient. And even though doubt often makes it difficult to follow; impatience for quick results makes other programs tempting; and inability to see the relevance to the ultimate goal of the daily tasks he sets me, makes life sometimes seem meaningless; yet I am content to hold to him and to be held by him.

D.T. NILES

A DISTANT LAMP

While I lay in that quiet front bedroom, with a distant street lamp throwing a reassuring glow through the curtained window, I began to think of the viciousness of people who would bomb my home. I could feel the anger rising when I realized that my wife and baby could have been killed. I thought about the city commissioners, and all the statements they had made about me and the Negro generally. I was once more on the verge of corroding hatred. And once more I caught myself and said: "You must not allow yourself to become bitter."

MARTIN LUTHER KING, JR.

REPENTANCE

We have to repent of our blindness, our lukewarmness and our disobedience, and turn back to our central truth of Christ as Lord and Saviour; an ethical system will not save us here; nor a timid sentimentalism; nor an excited emotional return or a dilettante mysticism.

We have to find that deep contrition which is the condition of His abiding.

Repentance is not a mere feeling of sorrow or contrition for an act of wrongdoing. The regret I feel when I act impatiently or speak crossly is not repentance. 'Contrition without repentance is a feeder of pride.' Repentance is contrition for what we are in our fundamental beings, that we are wrong in our deepest roots because our interior government is by Self and not by God.

And it is an activity of the whole person. Unless I will to be different the mind will not follow.

True repentance brings an urge to be different, because of the sense of the incessant movement of what I am, forming, forming, forming what I shall be in the years to come.

FLORENCE ALLSHORN

A NEW HEAVEN AND A NEW EARTH

This work of ours toward a new heaven and a new earth shows a correlation between the material and the spiritual, and, of course, recognizes the primacy of the spiritual. Food for the body is not enough. There must be food for the soul. Hence the leaders of the work, and as many as we can induce to join us, must go daily to Mass, to receive food for the soul. And as our perceptions are quickened, and as we pray that our faith be increased, we will see Christ in each other, and we will not lose faith in those around us, no matter how stumbling their progress is. It is easier to have faith that God will support each House of Hospitality and Farming Commune and supply our needs in the way of food and money to pay bills, than it is to keep a strong, hearty, living faith in each individual around us—to see Christ in him. If we lose faith, if we stop the work of indoctrinating, we are in a way denying Christ again.

We must practice the presence of God. He said that when two or three are gathered together, there He is in the midst of them. He is with us in our kitchens, at our tables, on our breadlines, with our visitors, on our farms. When we pray for our material needs, it brings us close to His humanity. He, too, needed food and shelter. He, too, warmed His hands at a fire and lay down in a boat to sleep.

When we have spiritual reading at meals, when we have the rosary at night, when we have study groups, forums, when we go out to distribute literature at meetings, or sell it on the street corners, Christ is there with us. What we do is so little we may seem to be constantly failing. But so did He fail. He met with apparent failure on the Cross. But unless the seed fall into the earth and die, there is no harvest.

And why must we see results? Our work is to sow. Another generation will be reaping the harvest.

DOROTHY DAY

THE ONLY WAY THAT WORKS

Love is not merely a weapon. It is not a strategy, and it may or may not work. To do good to those who hate you is such stupendous folly it can't be expected to work. Love didn't work for Jesus. No man has ever loved as he loved, but it didn't work. He wound up on a cross. And yet, it does work if your motive is not to make it work. Love works in the home. But if you say, "Well, you know, it really works to love your wife. If you love her, she'll darn your socks and bake you pie every day." If that is the motive for love, I doubt that your wife will darn your socks or bake pies. But love does work. I think Abraham Lincoln said it so well one day. Congressman Thaddeus Stevens, a bitter man from Massachusetts, shared the sentiment in the North to just crush the South after the war was over. When Mr. Lincoln was advocating binding up the wounds of the nation, and ideas such as forgiveness,

74

reconciliation, Thaddeus Stevens pounded the table and said, "Mr. Lincoln! I think enemies ought to be destroyed!" Mr. Lincoln quietly said, "Mr. Stevens, do not I destroy my enemy when I make him my friend?"

In the long run, it is the only way that really does work. For when the cards are all in, and the final chapter of history is written, when time is rolled up as a garment, and God is all and in all—on that final day, it will be the peacemakers, not the warriors, who will be called the Sons of God. . . .

Don't tell me Jesus didn't know about enemies that were bad and unlovable. He knew them quite well. He knew what they'd do to you. He knew they'd come out and hang you on a cross if you loved 'em. But he still says you're going to have to love them.

I don't know how we reconcile this with our attitudes to-day. "Well, you love these Russians, they're going to come over here and kill you and take your country." I don't know. Maybe they will. The first Christians had it pretty rough and I don't know that he can promise anything better than that to us. There is such a thing, though, as keeping good will in a very difficult situation. Last fall, several of my friends were arrested in Americus. One of the young fellows was from Koinonia. He was a Jewish lad. He had been working at Koinonia helping us to organize a farmer's co-operative for Negro farmers. And he was walking down the street of Americus and the police laid their hands on him, along with three others, threw him in jail, and charged all four with insurrection. There's an old law in Georgia that makes insurrection a capital offense. He was held in jail four or five months without bond because his offense was one that was punishable by death. During that time we tried to stay in communication with him by smuggling letters in and out through a trusty. On one occasion this young Jewish lad wrote a letter in which he intimated that his life was in great danger—not from the prison authorities but from his cellmates. The sheriff constantly reminded these cellmates that this boy was what he called "a nigger lover."

Now I want to quote from this Jewish boy because it reminds me so much of another Jewish young fellow who said almost the same thing, many many years ago. This is a quotation from a letter that came forth on a little piece of crumpled brown wrapping paper that he had written and wadded up and passed to the trusty. The trusty passed it to someone else and it was finally delivered a few days later.

"Though there is now no immediate threat, there have been challenges to fight and the danger will probably recur. I won't hit back under any circumstances. I want so badly to live and to get out of here, but if I am killed, perhaps I can still dry some tears and bring some joy. If I die, please see to it that my eyes or any other organs or parts of my body that can be used for transplants or other medical uses are donated to those uses. Then, please bury what's left of my body as it is without any box or coffin or any of that stuff, or embalming or fancy clothes other than what happens to be on the body, and then bury it at Koinonia. Just please plant a tree, a plum or a fig or a peach or a pecan, something that bears sweet fruit and has a long life, so that it may use what remains of my body to make pleasures for the children of my brothers here in Sumter County. Please see to it that no revenge or punishment or prosecution is taken against those of my brothers who have struck me down, but only that Sumter County officials be enjoined from putting a man ever again, no matter of what heinous crime accused, in the exposed position I'm in here. Thank you so much. May you all be blessed."

He does not bear the name of Christ, but he surely bears the spirit of a noble Jew who had seen that one must love his enemies regardless of what that enemy does.

It seems to me that we Christians have an idea here that the world is tremendously in need of. When we're tottering fearfully on the brink of utter annihilation, looking so desperately for hope from somewhere, walking in deep darkness, looking for one little streak of light, do not we Christians have some light? Can't we say, "Sure, we know the way. It's the way of love and of peace. We shall not confront the world with guns in our hands and bombs behind our backs. We shall confront the world without fear, with utter helplessness except for the strength of God."

CLARENCE JORDAN

A MAN WHO DOES EVERYTHING AT THE WRONG TIME

Is there any commission more terrible for a man than to have to announce the defeat of his own nation? to preach submission to the conqueror? to make himself disgraced as a traitor to his country?[1]

For Jeremiah this was not the point; God had given his verdict; the only repentance possible consists in the acceptance of this sentence. And in this act of acceptance lies their salvation. He knows, with the certitude which only a prophet can possess, that Babylon is the scourge of the Lord, meant to beat the nations as the corn is beaten upon the threshing floor—in order to sift the grain and disengage it from the straw. Against this tribunal, before which all nations will have to appear, no one can do anything. The cup of judgment is poured out; it must be drunk.[2]

But when everyone in the besieged city had lost heart, it was the prophet who bought a field, a sign of his certainty of future deliverance.[3]

Thus the prophet always looks like a man who does everything at the wrong time: he is a prophet of unhappiness in the midst of security; he denounces the false peace which is really only slavery;[4] he is the prophet of deliverance and of pardon at the height of the storm of disaster.[5]

For his views are the views of God, not of men. His gaze pierces the crust of appearances, and discovers the hidden meaning of history, of this history which God is writing with, and in spite of, men, whose final word will be resurrection and deliverance. He weighs men and events with something of the freedom of God himself. But to the extent in which God speaks through his mouth, he bleeds—with a sorrow which is both human and divine.

This was Jeremiah, the Prophet of the nations. . . .

SUZANNE de DIETRICH

[1] Jer. 37; 38.   [4] Jer. 6:13-14.
[2] Jer. 25:15-33.   [5] Jer. 31:1-6.
[3] Jer. 32:6-15.

A MORE CONVENIENT SEASON

Of course, there is nothing new about this kind of civil disobedience. It was evidenced sublimely in the refusal of Shadrach, Meshach and Abednego to obey the laws of Nebuchadnezzar, on the ground that a higher moral law was at stake. It was practiced superbly by the early Christians, who were willing to face hungry lions and the excruciating pain of chopping blocks rather than submit to certain unjust laws of the Roman Empire. To a degree, academic freedom is a reality today because Socrates practiced civil disobedience. In our own nation, the Boston Tea Party represented a massive act of civil disobedience.

We should never forget that everything Adolf Hitler did in Germany was "legal" and everything the Hungarian freedom fighters did in Hungary was "illegal." It was "illegal" to aid and comfort a Jew in Hitler's Germany. Even so, I am sure that, had I lived in Germany at the time, I would have aided and comforted my Jewish brothers. If today I lived in a Communist country where certain principles dear to the Christian faith are suppressed, I would openly advocate disobeying that country's antireligious laws.

I must make two honest confessions to you, my Christian and Jewish brothers. First, I must confess that over the past few years I have been gravely disappointed with the white moderate. I have almost reached the regrettable conclusion that the Negro's great stumbling block in his stride toward freedom is not the White Citizen's Counciler or the Ku Klux Klanner, but the white moderate, who is more devoted to "order" than to justice; who prefers a negative peace which is the absence of tension to a positive peace which is the presence of justice; who constantly says: "I agree with you in the goal you seek, but I cannot agree with your methods of direct action"; who paternalistically believes he can set the timetable for another man's freedom; who lives by a mythical concept of time and who constantly advises the Negro to wait for a "more convenient season." Shallow understanding from people of good will is more frustrating than absolute misunderstanding from people of

ill will. Lukewarm acceptance is much more bewildering
than outright rejection.

MARTIN LUTHER KING, JR.

ITINERANT PROPHETS

I am not surprised that most prophets are itinerants. Critics
of the church think we preachers are afraid to tell the truth
because we are economically dependent upon the people of
our church. There is something in that, but it does not quite
get to the root of the matter. I certainly could easily enough
get more money than I am securing now, and yet I catch
myself weighing my words and gauging their possible effect upon this and that person. I think the real clue to the
tameness of a preacher is the difficulty one finds in telling
unpleasant truths to people whom one has learned to love.

To speak the truth in love is a difficult, and sometimes
an almost impossible, achievement. If you speak the truth
unqualifiedly, that is usually because your ire has been
aroused or because you have no personal attachment to
the object of your strictures. Once personal contact is established you are very prone to temper your wind to the shorn
sheep. It is certainly difficult to be human and honest at the
same time. I'm not surprised that most budding prophets are
tamed in time to become harmless parish priests.

At that, I do not know what business I have carping at the
good people who are doing the world's work and who are
inevitably enmeshed to a greater or less degree in the ini-
quities of society. Conscience, Goethe has observed, belongs to the observer rather than the doer, and it would be
well for every preacher to realize that he is morally sensitive
partly because he is observing and not acting. What is satisfying about the ministry is to note how far you can go in un-
folding the full meaning of the Christian gospel provided you
don't present it with the implication that you have attained
and are now laying it as an obligation upon others.

If the Christian adventure is made a mutual search for

truth in which the preacher is merely a leader among many searchers and is conscious of the same difficulties in his own experience which he notes in others, I do not see why he cannot be a prophet without being forced into itinerancy.

REINHOLD NIEBUHR

WHAT DO YOU KNOW ABOUT HUNGER?

The pot is boiling because somebody makes it boil.
African proverb.

On a dark and icy cold morning in January 1946 I flew in an R.A.F. plane from Berlin to Kiel and then drove in a jeep to a British Army Church House a few miles outside the city. We passed through what had been the city centre but now the main street was a narrow, bumpy lane and the sides piled up with rubble. All round us were stark-naked ruins and such people as there were about were white-faced and grim. A man was searching in the filth for cigarette ends. Outside the city we passed by a refugee camp where white-faced, unsmiling boys and girls gazed at us through the railings. The next morning I looked out of the window of my warm bedroom into the backyard and saw a child enter the open gate from the garden, look cautiously round, lift the lid from an overflowing garbage bin and quickly and efficiently pick out the scraps of bread and other left-over from our supper tables the previous night. She ran off with the break-fast for her respectable middle-class family. I have never forgotten that little girl. This was what war had done to in-nocent children, not only had it starved them of food but reduced them to be scavengers.

I thought of her in 1955 when I was in Kenya at the height of the Mau Mau and saw hungry children huddled in corners of African huts. They were afraid of us until we managed to reassure them. Their parents had been taken off to detainee camps, and they were lonely and desolate. She came into my mind when a woman in the slums of West Kingston, Ja-maica, with a child at her breast and another three hanging around her skirts followed me around for two hours repeating, 'some milk would be better than nothing'.

She was there again when I helped in a feeding centre in Seoul in Korea, when the people came from broken-down shacks once a day to get soup and rice. Walking about at night in the streets of Calcutta and of necessity stepping over emaciated bodies too lethargic to move, or visiting refugee shacks in beautiful Hong Kong, or standing helplessly in the filthy slums of Kampala, always the same agony and anger assailed me as it did on that cold morning in Kiel. I asked myself each time, why can't I make the pot boil? It is easy for a well-fed English woman like myself to shake with anger about the futility of war, to protest verbally about the iniquity of racial prejudice and to deplore the helplessness of little people in the face of vast political forces fighting for power. It is less easy to take a full share of the blame and almost impossible to understand the feelings and aspirations of the legions of hungry people in the world.

I know nothing about hunger. I thought of that little girl last week when I nibbled some chocolates at a London theatre. The price of those chocolates would have paid for food for an Indian family for one day.

JANET LACEY

WHATSOEVER YOU DO

When in a prison, you came to my cell,
When on a sick bed, you cared for my needs,
In a strange country, you made me at home,
Seeking employment, you found me a job,
Hurt in a battle, you bound up my wounds,
Searching for kindness, you held out your hand,
When I was Negro, or Chinese, or White,
Mocked and insulted you carried my cross,

When I was aged, you bothered to smile,
When I was restless, you listened and cared.

You saw me covered with spittle and blood,
You knew my features, though grimy with sweat.

When I was laughed at, you stood by my side.
When I was happy, you shared in my joy.

MOTHER TERESA

THE SILENT, HUNGRY ONES

There is always silence in those who do not have the right or the courage to speak out in defense of undeniable rights, human rights.

Those who cannot earn bread for their families, those who must sleep on an empty stomach, those forced to listen to their children crying with hunger, either turn to extremism and violence or lapse into fear, cowardice, silence.

In comfortable—even luxurious—homes, someone may say: "I'm starving." Of course, those who say that do not know what they are saying. They are not hungry in any real sense. They should see the cities of the poor world, see how women, children and sometimes men, too, gather where the garbage bins are emptied.

Are they scavengers? They are looking for food, even food gone bad. They are looking for what has been wasted and, if properly shared, would be enough for all.

A chart was recently published showing the hunger areas of the United States. Amazing! The richest country in the world, the country that sends food surpluses all over the world to prevent domestic market upsets and falling farm prices, fails to provide food for a significant proportion of its children.

Protestants and Catholics attend banquets to raise funds to feed North American schoolchildren.

Hunger can cause physical distortions (not only in Biafra), mental distortions (how much mental retardation is caused by hunger!), moral distortion (the begging mentality), but above all, hunger nourishes silence.

When shall we have the courage to outgrow the charity mentality and see that at the bottom of all relations between rich and poor there is a problem of justice?

When shall we have enough understanding to recognize the urgency of employment (and not mere sub-employment) for every family head—employment that means life at a human, not subhuman, level?

DOM HELDER CÁMARA

NOTE: Every day, up to 10,000 children die of hunger in the world, and of sixty million deaths registered every year, one-third are due to hunger or its consequences.

Only 20 per cent of the world population has the necessary minimum daily intake of calories and proteins, whereas eighty per cent suffer chronic undernourishment or acute hunger. In the Northeast of Brazil, half of the population has not available more than 1600 calories daily.

THE WORLD NEEDS SAINTS

Compared to the vastness of what is needed, what we are able to do to serve others is so very insignificant. But let this bit of mutual help always be a sign of love.

In our work and on all occasions of our daily life we need to avoid pushing ourselves forward as if we ought to be doing better than the others. We are, and must remain, ordinary beings on the level of work, of effectiveness, and we ought to know that the extraordinary remains hidden: the invisible demand for holiness.

The people the world is needing are those men who are exceptional for the attention they give because they love. It is saints that the world is waiting for. Such is the secret appeal which rises from the depths of the sufferings of mankind.

Some women, who by their vocation live out this silent presence in a factory, told me that they could not remain unconscious of the advances which were renewed each day by this or that workmate: 'We are constantly being contaminated by the kind of life we live; hence the necessity to have a thirst for the salvation which God gives—for oneself and for others. And one of them added: 'May Christ help me to be converted each day together with them all.'

Only such a demand for holiness is capable of fitting us to live in surroundings on which fall darkness and the shadow of death. More than ever the world has need of saints. In the night of our world there must be men and women like a light of the world, and being this not so much because of their natural as by their supernatural equalities. 'In the depths of my life I can only live from Christ, from a single love—the love of God.' This is how one of these Christian women, who are committed to a difficult life in a factory with all its daily immoralities, expressed herself in a conversation with us.

ROGER SCHUTZ

NEW SAINTS

The faithful are told: "God is in the desert. You must separate yourself from the world and enter into solitude if you want to find God. God is in silence; if you want to hear him, you must flee the noise of the world. Only through contemplation can you know God, and an active life destroys contemplation. Forget the preoccupations of the world, for they are obstacles to an encounter with God."

But the layman lives in the midst of noise, surrounded by crowds, overwhelmed by necessary activities. He works in an office, surrounded by employees, and pores over columns of figures. He works in a factory, noise is everywhere, and he is the slave of a machine which becomes like a part of himself. He is packed into a bus, jammed into a subway. He is in an apartment whose paper-thin walls bring him the sounds of the lives of his neighbors. He is in a kitchen, always a little behind in washing the clothes, washing the vegetables, bathing the baby, getting the children off to school. He is at the beach, in a restaurant, in front of the television set. He is always busy, always worried—about the end-of-the-month bills, about the shoes he must buy, about a repairman for the washing machine, about the expenses he must meet, about the stock market. He belongs to a family and to a social *milieu;* he lives in a neighborhood, in a city, in a nation. He belongs to a union and goes to innumerable meetings. He agitates, struggles, fights for various movements and groups. *He is a part of life.* And yet, we tell him that he must separate himself from life if he is to find God. . . .

If God is truly present only "in the desert" and in silence, then he is not accessible to the majority of men today. And in that case, if the purpose of the Incarnation was to join Christ to man in the whole of life, we may say that the Incarnation has been a fiasco.

Fortunately, that is not the case. We know—through the words of a certain number of Christians—that the Holy Spirit is in the process of teaching us anew today that, although the gifts and vocations of each man are different, every man is called to meet Jesus and to unite himself to Jesus within the framework of that human life to which Providence has assigned him. The Holy Spirit is telling us that life today —like life yesterday—is not a "punishment"; it is a gift of love from the Creator. It is not an obstacle to divine union; it is the customary place for a meeting with Christ. Man is not condemned to live as "an exile" in this "valley of tears"; he is invited to participate, as a friend and a brother, in the mission entrusted to Jesus by the Father. It may be that participation has become burdensome and painful; if so, it is not by God's will but by man's sin, for its essential characteristic is the infinite joyfulness of the Resurrection.

We may be certain that, guided by the Holy Spirit, the laity will give to the Church those new saints of which she has such need. And, in the meantime, we must, with our brother laymen, search, pray, and live the adventure of sanctity in new ways.

MICHEL QUOIST

A NEW SAINTLINESS

Today it is not nearly enough merely to be a saint, but we must have the saintliness demanded by the present moment, a new saintliness, itself also without precedent.

Maritain said this, but he only enumerated the aspects of

saintliness of former days, which, for the time being at least, have become out of date. He did not feel all the miraculous newness the saintliness of today must contain in compensation.

A new type of sanctity is indeed a fresh spring, an invention. If all is kept in proportion and if the order of each thing is preserved, it is almost equivalent to a new revelation of the universe and of human destiny. It is the exposure of a large portion of truth and beauty hitherto concealed under a thick layer of dust. More genius is needed than was needed by Archimedes to invent mechanics and physics. A new saintliness is a still more marvelous invention

Only a kind of perversity can oblige God's friends to deprive themselves of having genius, since to receive it in superabundance they only need to ask their Father for it in Christ's name.

Such a petition is legitimate, today at any rate, because it is necessary. I think that under this or any equivalent it is the first thing we have to ask for now; we have to ask for it daily, hourly, as a famished child constantly asks for bread. The world needs saints who have genius, just as a plague-stricken town needs doctors. Where there is a need there is also an obligation.

SIMONE WEIL

CHURCH
AND
WORLD

3 CHURCH AND WORLD

CHURCH AND WORLD

What could not be placed under this category? The important thing here is the connective "and." For too long the choice seemed to be church *or* world, but that was always a false distinction. While Jesus warned us to be in but not of this world, he spent his life in witnessing to the world and died for it. For the world is not some abstraction, evil or good, but is made up of the whole human family. It is this that we talk about when we say "world", not a miscellany of governments or occasion for sin or an uninhabited nature or various political and economic systems, ours or others.

Early in 1973 an ecumenical gathering of Christians in Asia studied the theme Salvation Today. "Salvation is the central message of the Christian faith. It is the theme of the Bible," the preliminary booklet published by the World Council of Churches said. "For Christians, salvation is in Jesus Christ; yet his salvation is for all men, neither the word nor the hope of salvation belong to Christians alone. It is also the theme of contemporary songs and plays. Men and women of all kinds, in every land, use the word salvation and hope for it."

The church believes that God has acted and still acts. Through the Holy Spirit God is at work in the world today, accomplishing his purpose of salvation. To demonstrate this salvation, to discern those places where the spirit is at work is the task of the church. For the church is not something set completely against the world and over and apart from it. It is an instrument of God to serve the world and point to salvation. Above all the church is not a place to hide from the world and its problems but a loving community where grace and salvation are proclaimed.

Recently a sociological survey of attitudes of church members towards racial justice revealed that those most active in the quest for equality were also those who were most deeply involved in devotional practices. Far from being remote and otherworldly, those with the most intimate relationship to God through prayer and contemplation were also those who were most concerned for others. Compared with various forms of participation in church life in terms of organization, religious knowledge, belief and devotional practices made more difference in attitudes toward racial justice than any of the others. Or to put it our way, those who most love God most love others.

STRANGE COMMUNION

The Lord's Prayer is a we-prayer and only in this way also an I-prayer. "We" are the Church. The Church is the particular people, the congregation, or in Calvin's term, the company, which through a bit of knowledge of the gracious God manifest in Jesus Christ is constituted, appointed, and called as His witness in the world. This knowledge is paltry indeed, but because it is established by the Holy Spirit, it is unconquerable.

What is the existence of this particular people but the reflection of the humanity of God, although it is admittedly everywhere blurred and darkened and in its continuity all too often interrupted? This turning of God to man calls out and awakens some to worship, praise, and serve Him — many of them for the time being as representative of others and as His messengers to them. We should be inhuman where God is human, we should be ashamed of Jesus Christ Himself, were we willing to be ashamed of the Church. What Jesus Christ is for God and for us, on earth and in time, He is as Lord of this community, as King of this people, as Head of this body and of all its members. He is all these with and in this inconspicuous, painfully divided, and otherwise very questionable Christendom. He is all these with, among, and in the Christians whom one can admire or even love only in the face of many serious difficulties. He is all these—the Reconciler and Redeemer of the whole world. He is all these, however, in the strange communion of these strange saints. The Church is not too mean a thing for Him but, for better or for worse, sufficiently precious and worthy in His eyes to be entrusted with His witnessing and thus His affairs in the world—yes, even Himself. So great is God's loving-kindness!

KARL BARTH

THE WORLD IS REAL

Today, as throughout history, the world is something very real to believers. Their Bible, one might say, comes out of it.

In the world, God has made Himself known, first through the prophets and then, as Christians believe, through the presence of His Son. The world is thus a very special focus of God's action, from the beginning to the end of time. It stands for that excellent creation upon which the eyes of Love rested, which He found good, which He blessed with a mounting wave of life that culminated in consciousness, in man. And because God has found it good, the world continues to witness to the glory of God in a way that cannot finally be defaced or obscured. Creation is an ordered work of the divine wisdom and beauty. God's power shines through it; it is charged with His grandeur, the poet says. So man is awakened to acts of admiration and praise; he responds to God in and through the contemplation of His world.

And he turns to his fellow men and discovers himself anew in them. Indeed, apart from others, his knowledge risks delusions and emptiness, and his capacity for love hangs in the void. Man is created to know and love not only God but men.

DANIEL BERRIGAN

MOST OF US DO NOT LOVE PEOPLE

The individual sentimentalist is still with us even in the Church. If it is true, as I believe, that unity is of the foremost importance, then surely united action for the hungry world is an essential manifestation of the teachings of Jesus. The sentimentalists are generally speaking to be found in greater numbers outside the Church and it really is a form of arrogance and egoism that to me is intolerable. Whenever anyone says to me "but you see, I love people," I shudder. It is manifestly untrue or at best, superficial. It usually means an attitude of paternalism or a form of therapy for overwrought men and women. I feel compelled to support those who are struggling to ensure that people of all sorts get what is their right and that they are treated with compassion and love. 'I love people' rarely means that, although in any one day of my life the most exciting thing that can happen is

94

to meet someone alive and interesting who either inflates my mind or enriches my spirit: it is a sad truth that most of us do not 'love people' but just the reverse.

The second consideration, still with me, was the motive. Was it Christian? I do not know. Something had to be done and I did it without considering why. When asked by Christopher Chataway on a television programme whether I had felt called by God to be compelled to do compassionate work for those in need, I said 'No, not that I am aware of' because I had never understood what that question meant. I was criticised for giving that answer, and in reply I asked whether my critics would rather I had told a lie.

I think I can claim to be a religious person at least in thought if not in deed, and I am an almost fanatical believer in the ecumenical movement in the deepest meaning of the word. The world desperately needs unity. I believe that Jesus taught the love for mankind that knows no bounds and that the Church or its equivalent is an essential body in any country. It is a necessity in our culture and part of our history even if it is not any more accepted as an essential of life by the majority of the population. I have always found the dogmas and generally accepted doctrines of the Church difficult to accept and mostly impossible to believe. But, even when I have felt isolated and most bored by the Church, I have never been able to disassociate myself from religion and the quest for truth and the meaning of life. Who could not believe in the humanity of Jesus and all that he taught about love and peace? That the Church has allowed me to be its servant, to expound what I think the teaching of Jesus demands for suffering man and has given me its protection in spite of this, has never failed to move me to the depths. I go all the way with the much-quoted sentence from a book by Bertrand Russell at the time of his death: 'Remember your humanity and forget the rest. If you can do so, the way lies open to a new paradise: if you cannot, nothing lies before you but universal death.'

It is ironic that as the quest for unity goes forward the Church and the official ecumenical organizations become more institutionalized and so often irrelevant in this day and age. The language, the narrowness of those obsessed with institutional affairs, the fear that prevents leaders being honest about their doubts and the growing gap between ordinary people and the Church is tragic. But if man has to die to have lived, then I suppose the Church must do the same. What is unchanging is that others within and without the Church as well as I are in pursuit of truth and the less they believe the more they need the love and freedom that Jesus taught. This compulsion is of course to be found in other cultures and religions and among humanists. Their adherents face the same dilemmas.

How can I escape, but how can any of us assess our motives for what we do? I do not know. But a significant feature of society today is the fact that the Churches together have done, and are doing, more for suffering humanity than almost any other institution and this is true to their calling. But even more significant is the increasing compulsion of ordinary men and women, including young people, living in an increasingly sophisticated world, who while unable to accept the Christian faith in a 'package deal' or as a philosophy of life, are in large numbers occupied with caring for the refugees, the persecuted, the homeless and all in need. If it is true that God is everywhere whether we are there or not, or believe it or not, then whether their motives are Christian or not is of secondary importance. What to me is of primary importance is that I should continue the search, and refute with all the power and anger that I can muster, the inhuman barriers raised between man and man whatever the cause, different backgrounds of class, pseudo-intellectualism, religion, the colour of a man's skin, the ease with which nations resort to war, or the inhumanity of man caused by selfishness and the pursuit of power.

JANET LACEY

THE 60 AND THE 940

If, in imagination, we were to compress the present population of the world, now more than three billion, into a group of a thousand persons living in a single town, the brutal contrasts of affluence and destitution, of comfort and horrifying need, would be vivid indeed. Thus 60 persons would represent the American segment of the town, 940 the bulk of the world population. The 60 Americans would control half the total income of the town; the 940 would share, as best they could, the other half. The 60 Americans would have an average life expectancy of seventy-one years; all others in the town would die, on the average, before forty. The 60 Americans would enjoy fifteen times as much of all material goods as the rest of the townspeople on the average. They would produce 16 percent of the total food supply, would consume 14 percent of it, and would keep most of the remaining 2 percent in storage. The 60 Americans would, moreover, control and use twenty-one times as much petroleum as the others, twelve times as much electric power, twenty-two times as much coal, fifty times as much steel. The lowest-income groups among the 60 Americans would be better off, on the average, than most of the other townspeople. The contrast of wealth and poverty in our world would widen out in ever-larger areas of misery. Literally, most of the non-Americans would be poor, hungry, sick, and ignorant. Almost half would be unable to read or write.

In the light of all this, it remains quite probable that a renewal of the sense of poverty in the Church will always depend in large measure on the sense of their own life and times that believers have grasped. The age is past—if, indeed, it was ever present—when men could be effectively poor in spirit and remain at a distance from the fate of the majority of men. And when we consider man's fate today, it is clear that it ranges through a very wide spectrum of destitution, from the obvious and degrading kinds in the underdeveloped countries to the less conspicuous but omnipresent poverty of the slums of our great cities. A sense of this universal suffering, of such extent and implication as to beggar description, cannot but color a sense of what the vow of religious poverty is all about; it would bring home to believers the fact that there can be no such thing in the Church as an impersonal or apersonal poverty that would presume to please God.

DANIEL BERRIGAN

LET'S PRAY FOR THE SILENT WORLD

Father,

how can we not include
the whole of humanity
in our prayer,
because
your divine son,
our brother
Jesus Christ,
shed his blood
for all men,
everywhere,
at all times?

But, Lord,
allow me
my special concern
for my people,
the silent world.
There are
thousands
upon thousands
of human beings
in the poor countries,
and the poor regions
of the rich countries,
without the right
to speak out,
unable to complain,
to protest,
however just
their claims.

Those
without homes,
without food,
without garments,
without health,
without a minimum

of educational prospects,
without work,
without future,
without hope;
these people
risk falling
into fatalism.
They lose heart
and they lose
their voice.

If we,
who believe in you,
belonging
to the different
religions,
had helped
our privileged brothers—
opening their eyes,
arousing
their consciences—
injustices
would not have gone
so far, and there
would not have been
such a glaring distance
between rich and poor;
not only between
individuals
and groups
but between
countries
and even continents.

Father,
do that
which we have
not been

and are not
able to do.
How difficult
to surmount
the limit
of expediencies,
of help,
of gifts,
of the social-
welfare philosophy,
and attain
the domain
of justice.
The privileged
become angry,
believe themselves
misjudged,
see subversion
and communism
in
the most democratic,
the most human
and the most Christian
gestures!

The fault is
at least partly
ours.
If the churches
only gave
some evidence
of freeing themselves
from the enmeshment
of money!
If we,
who demand
the conversion
of others,
only gave
a personal,

authentic example
of a deep,
inner conversion!
And if,
when speaking,
denouncing,
protesting,
we always achieved
the ideal of winning
by friendship and love
the right
to tell the truth!

What we demand
is already
so difficult:
if it does not
become evident that
we do not feel
contempt,
superiority or
aggressiveness;

if it does not
become clear that
only love
of our neighbor
through
love of God
binds us,
then we shall only
provoke confusion.
Father,
may we become
more and more one
with your son.
May Christ
see with our eyes,
hear with our ears,
speak with our lips.

And send,
Father,
your Spirit,
which alone
can renew
the face of the earth.
He alone
can shatter
those egoisms
which must disappear

so that
the unjust structures
that hold millions
in bondage
may fall away.
Your Spirit alone
can help us to build
a more human
and a more Christian
world.

DOM HELDER CÂMARA

IRRELEVANT CLUB?

But the judgment of God is upon the church as never before. If today's church does not recapture the sacrificial spirit of the early church, it will lose its authenticity, forfeit the loyalty of millions, and be dismissed as an irrelevant social club with no meaning for the twentieth century. Every day I meet young people whose disappointment with the church has turned into outright disgust.

MARTIN LUTHER KING, JR.

REDEMPTIVE POWER

I am really beginning to like the ministry. I think since I have stopped worrying so much about the intellectual problems of religion and have begun to explore some of its ethical problems there is more of a thrill in preaching. The real meaning of the gospel is in conflict with most of the customs and attitudes of our day at so many places that there is adventure in the Christian message, even if you only play around with its ideas in a conventional world. I can't say that I have done anything in my life to dramatize the conflict between the gospel and the world. But I find it increasingly interesting to set the two in juxtaposition at least in my mind and in the minds of others. And of course ideas may finally lead to action.

A young woman came to me the other day in——and told me that my talk on forgiveness in the C—— Church of that town several months ago has brought about a reconciliation between her mother and sister after the two had been in a feud for five years. I accepted the news with more outward than inward composure. There is redemptive power in the message! I could go on the new courage that came out of that little victory for many a month.

I think I am beginning to like the ministry also because it gives you a splendid opportunity to have all kinds of contacts with people in relationships in which they are at their best. You do get tired of human pettiness at times. But there is nevertheless something quite glorious about folks. That is particularly true when you find them bearing sorrow with real patience. Think of Mrs. —— putting up with that drunkard of a husband for the sake of her children—and having such nice children. One can learn more from her quiet courage than from many a book.

REINHOLD NIEBUHR

THE HONEST PATH

The honest path for us now is to admit that we are not the know-alls we have long pretended, and that for the tiny fragment of God which we have seen and which has made us indelible Christians—there is infinitely more that we have not seen and have not begun to guess at. We are like archaeologists pedantically reconstructing a civilization from one piece of pottery while a whole city lies buried beneath our feet.

But we not only need daring, but also naturalness and honesty. We have for so long adopted a special tone of voice for talking about God, a quaint style for religious buildings, religious writings, religious talking, even religious printing. (I remember one friend of mine who wanted to start a new religious publication and could not woo the printer away from gothic conceits.) And we have fallen time and time again into the disastrous habit of talking in ideals, so that Christians collected together do not talk of what they actually are thinking and feeling, but of what they *ought* to be thinking and feeling.

There is a great need for us to recognize that in worshipping God we are frequently ridiculous, and that it will not do for us to conceal this knowledge from ourselves with a show of pomposity and an air of false reverence. The incongruity between man and God, the sheer difference of scale, is probably the fundamental joke, the father and mother, the Alpha and Omega, of all the jokes in the world. It's a pity people don't laugh at it more often.

It seems to me that the pomposity of Western religion, its tendency to fear the emotions and the realities of personal life, and try to take refuge in administrative achievement, may have to do with its determined masculinity. I remember being told in my early days as a Christian that what I felt didn't matter, that what *did* matter was the will; a piece of nonsense which any woman could recognize immediately as nonsense. It is not by chance that the position of women in our churches is such an ambivalent one; comparatively few women care to assert themselves outside the purely practical sphere, because the Church so rarely seems to be arguing in their language or about issues which seem to them important. Church discussion tends to begin with abstractions and work down eventually, if it gets so far, to the individuals involved in the situation. A true femininity begins with personalities and works outwards to abstractions. It is the Church's loss that she has so long despised feminine insights which might have taken her instinctively and quickly to situations which she has reached only slowly and by elaborate reasoning.

MONICA FURLONG

ISRAEL BELIEVED IN MONEY

In every authentic vocation there is a mystery, known to no one, save God; he speaks to the heart of a man, and all that this man can do is to obey. The prophet is a man who is bound by the word of God:

'The lion hath roared, who will not fear?

The Lord God hath spoken, who can but prophesy?' [1]

But the divine inspiration does not act in a magical way. God had opened the mind and heart of Amos to his law, to his revelation, as it had already been given to his fathers. The God who speaks by the mouth of Amos is the one holy God proclaimed by Moses; the God who had delivered Israel from the yoke of Egypt,[2] and who had just given them victory over the Syrians; a God who is merciful to all who repent, terrible in his judgments; a God who cannot endure idolatry, who hates hypocrisy and lying; a righteous God, the one who is forever on the side of the oppressed, as their defender. . . .

But the way in which Amos denounces the *causes of the corruption of the nation* contains a warning which is valid for all nations. With prosperity Israel became in fact enslaved to the power of money; the vices of civilization, drunkenness, prostitution, have destroyed this people which was previously simple and unpolished. Formerly a people of shepherds, without separate classes, Israel now knows the extremes of great luxury and great poverty and misery. The women set the example: they lead their husbands to drink; they are hard on the poor who knock at the door; like the fat cattle of the Mesopotamian plains, they think of nothing save of enjoying themselves and getting fat.[3] When woman loses her dignity as woman, society soon rots. That was the case with Samaria.

Above all there is one word which is continually on the lips of Amos; righteousness (justice). There is no longer any justice in the land. The judges let themselves be bought. That also is a sign of the decadence of a nation; and especially of a nation which had received the Law from God himself.

For all these corruptions spring from one sin, which lies at the root of all the others; Israel had ceased to believe in the living God, Israel believed in money, pleasure, success.

SUZANNE de DIETRICH

1. Amos 3:8.   2.. Amos 2:10.   3. Amos 4:1.

DISPLACED PERSONS

Young people today have hardly ever heard of the concentration camps found all over Germany at the end of the Second World War, or of the horrifying and diabolical cruelty meted out to millions of men and women just because they were Jews. Every kind of torture was used on them, the like of which we have only read in descriptions of torture in the dark ages or have conjured up in our minds when looking at instruments of torture in the Tower of London. They were starved of food and lived under indescribable conditions, with their prison numbers branded on their arms and bodies with red-hot irons. They had to 'line up' to await their turn for the gas chambers. There were millions more who were not Jews but were in countries other than their own at the end of the war and unable to return because of changing political policies and borders. They were called Displaced Persons. Young people today quite rightly think that we must face the human problems of today and forget the past. But no history of the Churches' care for rejected and homeless people would be complete without recalling the years in the thirties and forties when so many men and women endured indescribable suffering. From the beginning and to the end of this prolonged crisis the Churches together were there to help and rescue them.

Whenever there is a mass movement of refugees, there are large numbers of children, often moving in groups or alone. There is nothing more tragic to gaze upon than one child dragging its feet, alone and yet determined to arrive somewhere. Children who survive such dreadful experiences have managed to do so because they have had to adjust themselves to unnatural and dangerous circumstances and tremendous hazards.

I saw and tried to talk to some of these children in large underground, dimly-lit bunkers in Hanover in 1945 and 1946. Some had been walking, mostly at night, for two years from one side of Germany to the other. They lived like animals and their faces were like those of old men and women of eighty. The social workers living in the bunkers had to stay below in the dark because the children were afraid of the light. What, I wonder, are they like today? How many children today are wandering on other continents because of cruel wars and persecution, and what can be done about it?

JANET LACEY

GREATLY DISAPPOINTED

Let me take note of my other major disappointment. I have been so greatly disappointed with the white church and its leadership. Of course, there are some notable exceptions. I am not unmindful of the fact that each of you has taken some significant stands on this issue. I commend you, Reverend Stallings, for your Christian stand on this past Sunday, in welcoming Negroes to your worship service on a non-segregated basis. I commend the Catholic leaders of this state for integrating Spring Hill College several years ago.

But despite these notable exceptions, I must honestly reiterate that I have been disappointed with the church. I do not say this as one of those negative critics who can always find something wrong with the church. I say this as a minister of the gospel, who loves the church; who was nurtured in its bosom; who has been sustained by its spiritual blessings and who will remain true to it as long as the cord of life shall lengthen.

When I was suddenly catapulted into the leadership of the bus protest in Montgomery, Alabama, a few years ago, I felt we would be supported by the white church. I felt that the white ministers, priests and rabbis of the South would be among our strongest allies. Instead, some have been outright opponents, refusing to understand the freedom movement and misrepresenting its leaders; all too many others have been more cautious than courageous and have remained silent behind the anesthetizing security of stained-glass windows.

In spite of my shattered dreams, I came to Birmingham with the hope that the white religious leadership of this community would see the justice of our cause and, with deep moral concern, would serve as the channel through which our just grievances could reach the power structure. I had hoped that each of you would understand. But again I have been disappointed.

I have heard numerous southern religious leaders admonish their worshipers to comply with a desegregation decision because it is the law, but I have longed to hear white ministers declare: "Follow this decree because integration is morally right and because the Negro is your brother." In the midst of blatant injustices inflicted upon the Negro, I have watched white churchmen stand on the sidelines and mouth pious irrelevancies and sanctimonious trivialities. In the midst of a mighty struggle to rid our nation of racial and economic injustice, I have heard many ministers say: "Those are social issues, with which the gospel has no real concern." And I have watched many churches commit themselves to a completely other-worldly religion which makes a strange un-biblical distinction between body and soul, between the sacred and secular.

MARTIN LUTHER KING, JR.

THE LONELIEST PEOPLE

Some of the loneliest people in our community are those who have failed in one way or another in the ideal code of behaviour we have laid down; the unmarried mother, the young man who has discovered that he is homosexual, the divorcee, the man or woman who is haunted by thoughts of suicide and may have made more than one attempt at it, the middle-aged man who has committed adultery. Would any of these people turn automatically to the local Christian community, in the confident expectation that they would receive love and understanding?

Some of these people might, and do, turn to a parish priest for comfort and help, or to some other Christian organization. But if the priest is to solve their loneliness permanently, and is to offer something more valuable than a clinging and dependent relationship upon himself, then he needs an accepting community into which he can introduce those who suffer acutely from a sense of exclusion.

A few churches have such a nucleus of people, but the majority of church-folk are not like that, partly because of an ignorance and a lack of imagination which oversimplifies moral behavior, partly because they fear that to forgive anti-social attitudes is to condone them. This is the old fear . . . that truth will not prevail, that the moral structure of a nation is so fragile that it needs elaborate defenses. Christians, it seems to me, have to choose between the safety of "morals" and the danger of love. It is my own belief that Christ's teaching was principally about the latter, but that if you do reach men and women to love God and love their neighbour then morals take care of themselves.

The literal loving of the neighbour is something preachers might mention much more often than they do. We are good at getting ourselves so immersed in the sea of religious metaphor that the obvious disappears. In our figurative vagueness we can manage to lose sight of the fact that we are supposed to love the people who live next door and that we have to solve our problems of relationship within our own marriages and with our own children. Love must be a process of learning to be vulnerable—to one another, to ideas, to knowledge, to the arts, even to the injuries which the forces of evil constantly try to inflict. It is impossible to love without getting hurt, if only because the loveless may be incapable of responding to love. This is what is meant about taking up the cross and following Christ. Being a Christian means believing that love overcomes lovelessness, though at a cost.

MONICA FURLONG

MY PEOPLE: THE SILENT SHACKS

Slums! At Olinda and Recife they're called mocambos, in Rio de Janeiro they are known as favelas. The poor countries and the poor regions of the wealthy countries have the same kind of hovels; they differ in name but share the same unvarying one aspect: they are not real homes, they form no effective political community. Those living in the hovels are silent, for even though they may speak, they are not heard.

The mocambos are noisy; transistor radios blare out football (soccer) commentaries, pop music, dramas; drunks bellow; neighbors gossip, argue, hurl insults; dogs bark and howl at the moon; cocks crow.

The mocambos are silent when the time comes to speak out for rights. Very often the mocambos have to be built in secret. Sometimes construction is authorized, but only with temporary materials, so as not to establish any permanence, any community, any rights. Improvements to the mocambos are nearly always forbidden.

And one day . . . a company comes along, buys land, does everything to get the occupants off, gives permission for the debris to be taken away. Sometimes it's not a corporation but the local authorities, wanting to beautify the city.

If anyone dares to speak out, to protest, then of course that's subversion and communism!

When will there be sufficient understanding that human beings have the right to a human home? When will it be realized that what makes a town ugly above all things is the lack of humanity? When will the silent voice of the mocambos be heard?

DOM HELDER CÁMARA

NOTE: Nine out of ten homes in Central American Honduras have no floors, only bare ground. Eight out of ten houses in Paraguay are without proper roofs. Only 4.5 per cent of all dwellings in Chile have running water, only 4.2 per cent of the houses in Colombia have electricity.

IDENTIFYING OURSELVES WITH THE POOR

An increasingly strong call to poverty is making itself felt among Christians. The younger generations are very hard on any suggestion of luxury. The strong criticism made by many young laymen springs from the right motives, but if we accept renunciation we must recognise that it is not restricted to material things. The fact of having limited means might lead us, without our knowing it, to look for a different form of security, for example by imposing ourselves on the minds of others, and forcing them to enter into our own way of seeing things. The spirit of poverty embraces the whole of our being. Outward signs of poverty are not enough; they still leave room for human ambition, the urge for power, and the desire to dominate one's neighbour, which outward appearances only disguise.

To put forward an ideal which is unattainable in an affluent society means that those who seek a life of poverty according to the Gospel are forced to live in a situation of continual tension; they want to attain the inaccessible. The aim of the Gospel is not to destroy personality, it is only trying to arouse a healthy discontent. To demand the impossible leads to critical situations. There are some demands which keep us locked up in inner conflicts. Are we not witnessing in certain cases the establishment of a new kind of Jansenism?

The vow of poverty itself, if it is aggressively asserted, not only enlightens no one but is destructive on account of the bitterness which it contains. A man or woman who has taken the vow of poverty must never forget the father and mother of a family who have children to care for. The demands of our life cannot be theirs. They can so easily become oppressive for them and prevent them from understanding our vows. Aggressive poverty arouses fear.

The spirit of poverty must not become hard; it must not become judging. We must not exalt one Beatitude at the expense of others. The poor man is gentle, he is the poor man of Yahweh, dependent at every moment on God alone.

In this sphere it is essential to maintain a just balance. Poverty is nothing without charity, a shadow without light. He who, in the name of poverty, makes a complacent condemnation of his neighbour, can be certain that he is in the wrong.

ROGER SCHUTZ

4

**LIFE AND
DEATH**

4 LIFE AND DEATH

LIFE AND DEATH

Is there a connection? Or is one only the absence of the other? Surely this question is at the heart of the Gospel. It has been suggested that as earlier generations avoided all mention of sex, ours has as its special taboo topic "death." We try to avoid considering it, to prolong life and disguise its approach, to shut away its reminders including old people who once had an honored place in the community and the family. This is not just true of the United States. See what the Russian Nobel prize winner novelist Alexander Solzhenitsyn says about the Soviet Union. In this section we encounter again witnesses, for Martin Luther King knew that death was imminent and that gave sharp meaning to his life. The teacher and musician Albert Schmidt-Sas who was killed by the Nazis reveals death to us as the "Zenith of Life." More commonplace and nearer to our experience are the accounts of three very different men: Joseph Mathews who heads the Chicago Ecumenical Institute, in his tale of his father's death; the account by moderator Suzuki of the United Church in Japan (the Kyodan), of his thoughts on learning that he is dying of cancer; and the piece by Claude Thompson, late of the Emory University's Candler School of Theology, on his last days. Even the church is not likely to talk much of death except in hushed tones at funerals. Its dynamic relationship to life, the ways in which we must face it, and its meaning are too often left for us to discover alone and with little preparation. In this section you will find many different approaches to the subject of life and death. There is the lawyer William Stringfellow who in the midst of a busy life found that he might soon die. There is his friend Melvin Schoonover, himself confined to a wheelchair from which he had to fight his way into the ministry and marriage and the world, as he tries to tell his daughter Polly about life. For Polly has inherited the disease which means that her brittle bones will break all her life. This whole little book *Letters to Polly,* on the meaning of affliction, has much to teach us of life.

ON HEALING

The physician can help, he can keep us alive, but can he make us whole? Can he give us salvation? Certainly not, if discord, cleavage, restlessness rule our mental life, if there is no unity and therefore no freedom in our soul, if we are possessed by compulsions and fantasies, by disordered anxiety and disordered aggression, if mental disorder or disease are threatening or have conquered us. Then if we want to be healed, we ask for the help of friends or counselors or analysts or psychiatrists. And they, if they know what to do, try to aid the healing powers of our soul. They do not appeal to our will power; they do not ask for removal or suppression of any trend, but they work for reconciliation, reconciliation of the struggling forces of our soul. They accept us as we are and make it possible for us to look at ourselves honestly and with clarity, to realize the strange mechanisms under which we are suffering and to dissolve them, reconciling the genuine forces of our soul with each other and making us free for thought and action.

The counselor and psychiatrist can *help;* he can liberate us, but can he make us whole? Can he give us salvation? Certainly not if we are not able to use our freedom and if we are conquered by the tragic conflicts of our existence. None of us is isolated. We belong to our past, to our families, classes, groups, nations, cultures. And in all of them health and illness are fighting with each other. How can we be whole if the culture is split within itself, if every value is denied by another one, if every truth is questioned, if every decision is good and bad at the same time? How can we be whole if the institutions in which we live create temptations, conflicts, catastrophes too heavy for each of us? How can we be whole if we are connected, often intimately connected with people who are in discord with themselves, in hostility against us, or if we have to live with people, individuals, groups, nations who are irreconciled and sick? This is the situation of all of us, and this situation reacts on our personal life, disrupts the concord we may have reached. The reconciliation in our souls and often even in our bodies breaks down in the encounter with reality. Who heals reality?

Who brings us a new reality? Who reconciles the conflicting forces of our whole existence? We look at those who are most responsible for our institutions, for our historical reality, the leaders, the statesmen, the wise administrators, the educated, the good people, the revolutionary masses. There are healing powers in all of them, otherwise there would be no more history. And it is understandable that in the period of Jesus just rulers were called saviors and healers. They can maintain human life on earth; but can they make us whole, can they bring us salvation?

They cannot because they themselves need wholeness and are longing for salvation. Who heals the healer? There is no answer to this in the old reality. Everybody and every institution are infected, the healer and the healed. Only a new reality can make us whole, breaking into the old one, reconciling it with itself. It is the humanly incredible, ecstatic, often defeated, but never conquered faith of Christianity that this new reality which was always at work in history, has appeared in fullness and power in Jesus, the Christ, the Healer and Savior. This is said of Him because He alone does not give another law for thought or action, because He does not cut off anything or suppress anything that belongs to life, but because He is the reality of reconciliation, because in Him a new reality has come upon us in which we and our whole existence are accepted and reunited. We know, even when we confess this faith, that the old reality of conflict and disease has not disappeared. Our bodies ail and die, our souls are restless, our world is a battlefield of individuals and groups. But the new reality cannot be thrown out. We live from it, even if we do not know it. For it is the power of reconciliation whose work is wholeness and whose name is love.

PAUL TILLICH

TAKING STUPID RISKS

I guess what I am saying is that what a man finds especially liberating is to act with integrity. It is assumed by most people that everyone's primary responsibility is to protect himself, to act out of self-interest, to trample if he can on those who are weaker or less astute. And that is precisely why the world is in such a mess.

People like us, Polly, never have any security. No one really has, but most people can prolong the illusion that they have. Catastrophe is always imminent for us. No matter how prudent and cautious and self-protective we are, we have no immunity against injury and pain and death. It is not even a reasonable option for us to withdraw from society to gain relative safety. Our bones can break almost as easily in the protection of home as on the street. Whatever tiny margin of safety can be gained through such draconian measures is bought at the price of living death. As Dr. Wilson once said to me, "There are worse things than broken legs."

In a funny kind of way we find our lives only by throwing them away, by taking all kinds of stupid risks not only to physical well-being but also to any self-centered notion that we can somehow be independent of other men. What I have been saying to you in these letters is that I have found my life through the acceptance of those risks, especially the risk of entrusting my life to encounter with all kinds of human beings. People marvel at my "independence," completely failing to see that my independence is a by-product of acknowledged inter-dependence. I have achieved freedom to give what I have because I have been willing to affirm how much others have given.

The willingness to be open, to trust, to approach others in freedom is perhaps a great contribution we can make to the world, Polly. Oh, I know, it is very hard to live like that. Sometimes the temptations are overpowering. The only way it is possible is to receive that constant "transfusion of grace" which, as I have said over and over in these letters, has come to us both when we least expected it and then from the most unlikely sources.

In that, I suppose, our experience parallels that of Jesus of Nazareth. Not only do I think his "style of life" is the only one I can rationally defend. More than that, his final victory over evil and suffering and death gives me hope that we— and all men—can and shall reach the "kingdom." There the physical burdens will be laid aside, and the walls of separation between human beings shall be torn down, and we shall all be free to love and live as God always intended us to do.

Good night, my beloved Polly.   *Daddy*

MELVIN E. SCHOONOVER

THE GREAT WORLD AND THE LITTLE WORLD

We all want to be certain, we all want proof, but the kind of proof that we tend to want—scientifically or philosophically demonstrable proof that would silence all doubts once and for all—would not in the long run, I think, answer the fearful depths of our need at all. For what we need to know, of course, is not just that God exists, not just that beyond the steely brightness of the stars there is a cosmic intelligence of some kind that keeps the whole show going, but that there is a God right here in the thick of our day-by-day lives who may not be writing messages about himself in the stars but who in one way or another is trying to get messages through our blindness as we move around down here knee-deep in the fragrant muck and misery and marvel of the world. It is not objective proof of God's existence that we want but, whether we use religious language for it or not, the experience of God's presence. That is the miracle that we are really after. And that is also, I think, the miracle that we really get.

I believe that we know much more about God than we admit that we know, than perhaps we altogether know that we know. God speaks to us, I would say, much more often than we realize or than we choose to realize. Before the sun sets every evening, he speaks to each of us in an intensely personal and unmistakable way. His message is not written out in starlight, which in the long run would make no difference; rather it is written out for each of us in the humdrum, helter-skelter events of each day; it is a message that in the long run might just make all the difference.

Who knows what he will say to me today or to you today or into the midst of what kind of unlikely moment he will choose to say it. Not knowing is what makes today a holy mystery as every day is a holy mystery. But I believe that there are some things that by and large God is always saying to each of us. Each of us, for instance, carries around inside himself, I believe, a certain emptiness—a sense that something is missing, a restlessness, the deep feeling that somehow all is not right inside his skin. Psychologists sometimes call it anxiety, theologians sometimes call it estrangement, but whatever you call it, I doubt that there are many who do not recognize the experience itself, especially no one of our age, which has been variously termed the age of anxiety, the lost generation, the beat generation, the lonely crowd. Part of the inner world of everyone is this sense of emptiness, unease, incompleteness, and I believe that this in itself is a word from God, that this is the sound that God's voice makes in a world that has explained him away. In such a world, I suspect that maybe God speaks to us most clearly through his silence, his absence, so that we know him best through our missing him.

But he also speaks to us about ourselves, about what he wants us to do and what he wants us to become; and this is the area where I believe that we know so much more about him than we admit even to ourselves, where people hear God speak even if they do not believe in him. A face comes toward us down the street. Do we raise our eyes or do we keep them lowered, passing by in silence? Somebody says something about somebody else, and what he says happens to be not only cruel but also funny, and everybody laughs. Do we laugh too, or do we speak the truth? When a friend has hurt us, do we take pleasure in hating him, because hate has its pleasures as well as love, or do we try to build back some flimsy little bridge? Sometimes when we are alone, thoughts come swarming into our heads like bees—some of them destructive, ugly, self-defeating thoughts, some of them creative and glad. Which thoughts do we choose to think then, as much as we have the choice? Will we be brave today or a coward today? Not in some big way probably but in some little foolish way, yet brave still. Will we be honest today or a liar? Just some little pint-sized honesty, but honest still. Will we be a friend or cold as ice today?

All the absurd little meetings, decisions, inner skirmishes

that go to make up our days. It all adds up to very little, and yet it all adds up to very much. Our days are full of nonsense, and yet not, because it is precisely into the nonsense of our days that God speaks to us words of great significance—not words that are written in the stars but words that are written into the raw stuff and nonsense of our days, which are not nonsense just because God speaks into the midst of them. And the words that he says, to each of us differently, are *be brave . . . be merciful . . . feed my lambs . . . press on toward the goal.*

But they are not all trivia and routine and nonsense, our lives. There are the crises too, crises that shake to the foundations both the great world of the nations and the little world of the individual. And we hear God speak through the crises too, many different kinds of words but sometimes, I think, a word quite different from the others. I am thinking of the great international crises that threaten the world itself with annihilation, and in terms of the individual, I am thinking of the deaths of people we love and of the failures and betrayals and of all that rises to imperil our inner peace.

In one of the last letters that St. Paul very likely ever wrote, a letter that he sent off from prison on his way to Rome and death, he has this to say at the end. "Rejoice in the Lord always; again I will say, Rejoice. The Lord is at hand. Have no anxiety about anything, but in everything by prayer and supplication with thanksgiving let your requests be known to God." And through the great crises of our times and through the little crises of each of our times, I believe that this is a deep part of what God says to us. Yes, take your times seriously. Yes, know that you are judged by the terrible sins of your times. Yes, you do well to faint with fear and foreboding at what is coming on the world. And yet rejoice. Rejoice. The Lord is at hand. Have no anxiety. Pray.

These words that God speaks to us in our own lives are the real miracles. They are not miracles that create faith as we might think that a message written in the stars would create faith, but they are miracles that it takes faith to see— faith in the sense of openness, faith in the sense of willingness to wait, to watch, to listen, for the incredible presence of God here in the world among us.

FREDERICK BUECHNER

TO WHOM MUCH IS FORGIVEN

As long as we feel rejected by Him, we cannot love God. He appears to us as an oppressive power, as He who gives laws according to His pleasure, who judges according to His commandments, who condemns according to His wrath. But if we have received and accepted the message that He *is* reconciled, everything changes. Like a fiery stream His healing power enters into us; we can affirm Him and with Him our own being and the others from whom we were estranged, and life as a whole. Then we realize that His love is the law of our own being, and that it is the law of reuniting love. And we understand that what we have experienced as oppresssion and judgment and wrath is in reality the working of love, which tries to destroy within us everything which is against love. To love this love is to love God. Theologians have questioned whether man is able to have love towards God; they have replaced love by obedience. But they are refuted by our story. They teach a theology for the righteous ones but not a theology for the sinners. He who is forgiven knows what it means to love God.

And he who loves God is also able to accept life and to love it. This is not the same as to love God. For many pious people in all generations the love of God is the other side of the hatred for life. And there is much hostility towards life in all of us, even in those who have completely surrendered to life. Our hostility towards life is manifested in cynicism and disgust, in bitterness and continuous accusations against life. We feel rejected by life, not so much because of its objective darkness and threats and horrors, but because of our estrangement from its power and meaning. He who is reunited with God, the creative Ground of life, the power of life in everything that lives, is reunited with life. He feels accepted by it and he can love it. He understands that the greater love is, the greater the estrangement which is conquered by it. In metaphorical language I should like to say to those who feel deeply their hostility towards life: Life accepts you; life loves you as a separated part of itself; life wants to reunite you with itself, even when it seems to destroy you.

There is a section of life which is nearer to us than any other and often the most estranged from us; other human beings. We all know about the regions of the human soul in which things look quite different from the way they look on its benevolent surface. In these regions we can find hidden hostilities against those with whom we are in love. We can find envy and torturing doubt about whether we are really accepted by them. And this hostility and anxiety about being rejected by those who are nearest to us can hide itself under the various forms of love: friendship, sensual love, conjugal and family love. But if we have experienced ultimate acceptance this anxiety is conquered, though not removed. We can love without being sure of the answering love of the other one. For we know that he himself is longing for our acceptance as we are longing for his, and that in the light of ultimate acceptance we are united.

He who is accepted ultimately can also accept himself. Being forgiven and being able to accept oneself are one and the same thing. No one can accept himself who does not feel that he is accepted by the power of acceptance which is greater than he, greater than his friends and counselors and psychological helpers. They may point to the power of acceptance, and it is the function of the minister to do so. But he and the others also need the power of acceptance which is greater than they. . . .

Decisive spiritual experiences have the character of a break-through. In the midst of our futile attempts to make ourselves worthy, in our despair about the inescapable failure of these attempts, we are suddenly grasped by the certainty that we are forgiven, and the fire of love begins to burn. That is the greatest experience anyone can have. It may not happen often, but when it does happen, it decides and transforms everything.

And now let us look once more at those whom we have described as the righteous ones. They are really righteous, but since little is forgiven them, they love little. And this is their unrighteousness. It does not lie on the moral level, just as the unrighteousness of Job did not lie on the moral level where his friends sought for it in vain. It lies on the level of the encounter with ultimate reality, with God who vindicates Job's righteousness against the attacks of his friends, with the God who defends Himself against the attacks of Job and his ultimate unrighteousness. The righteousness of the righteous ones is hard and self-assured. They, too, want forgiveness, but they believe that they do not need much of it. And so their righteous actions are warmed by very little love. They could not have helped the woman in our story, and they cannot help us, even if we admire them. Why do children turn from their righteous parents and husbands from their righteous wives, and vice versa? Why do Christians turn away from their righteous pastors? Why do people turn away from righteous neighborhoods? Why do many turn away from righteous Christianity and from the Jesus it paints and the God it proclaims? Why do they turn to those who are not considered to be the righteous ones? Often, certainly, it is because they want to escape judgment. But more often it is because they seek a love which is rooted in forgiveness, and this the righteous ones cannot give. Many of those to whom they turn cannot give it either. Jesus gave it to the woman who was utterly unacceptable. The Church would be more the Church of Christ than it now is if it did the same, if it joined Jesus and not Simon in its encounter with those who are rightly judged unacceptable. Each of us who strives for righteousness would be more Christian if more were forgiven him, if he loved more and if he could better resist the temptation to present himself as acceptable to God by his own righteousness.

PAUL TILLICH

NEW LIFE

We are so convinced that past evils must repeat themselves that we make them repeat themselves. We dare not risk a new life in which the evils of the past are totally forgotten; a new life seems to imply new evils, and we would rather face evils that are already familiar. Hence we cling to the evil that has already become ours, and renew it from day to day, until we become identified with it and change is no longer thinkable.

THOMAS MERTON

WE WILL NEVER DIE

Above all else, we have grown to fear death and those who die.

If there is a death in a family, we try to avoid writing or calling, because we do not know what to say about death.

It is even considered shameful to mention a cemetery seriously. You would never say at work: "Sorry, I can't come on Sunday, I've got to visit my relatives at the cemetery." What is the point of bothering about people who are not going to invite you to a meal?

What an idea—moving a dead man from one town to another! No one would lend a car for that. And nowadays, if you're a nonentity, you don't get a hearse and a funeral march—just a quick trip on a lorry.

Once people used to go to our cemeteries on Sundays and walk between the graves, singing beautiful hymns and spreading sweet-smelling incense. It set your heart at rest; it allayed the painful fears of inevitable death. It was almost as though the dead were smiling from under their grey mounds: "It's all right. . . . Don't be afraid."

But nowadays, if a cemetery is kept up, there's a sign there: "Owners of graves! Keep this place tidy on penalty of a fine!" But more often they just roll them flat with bulldozers, to build sports grounds and parks.

Then there are those who died for their native land—it could still happen to you or me. There was a time when the church set aside a day of remembrance for those who fell on the battlefield. England does this on Poppy Day. All nations dedicate one day to remembering those who died for us all.

More men died for us Russians than for any other people,

yet we have no such day. If you stop and think about the dead, who is to build the new world? In three wars we have lost so many husbands, sons, and lovers; yet to think of them repels us. They're dead, buried under painted wooden posts — why should they interfere with our lives? For we will never die!

ALEXANDER SOLZHENITSYN

TOMORROW

(Note: Moderator Suzuki's last message was tape recorded on June 26th, 1969, by Harue Yoshioka for the members of Nishi Katamachi Church, of which Mr. Suzuki was pastor, and is made available in print for the many who shared anxiety over his illness, in the hope that they may also be enabled to enter into his feelings. It constitutes one of three tapes that were recorded. The "Reiko" referred to is Mr. Suzuki's daughter. Translated from the Kyodan Times, July 19,1969, by Ian MacLeod.)

Each day in the hospital is a very busy one. Just now I have finished my lunch and, thank goodness, have a couple of hours' rest ahead of me. I haven't gathered my thoughts especially, but since there may be some who would like to hear my voice, I shall chat for a little.

From what the doctor told me the day before yesterday, my cancer began about two years ago. When I come to think of it, I have been aware frequently for the past two years of a certain physical listlessness and feverishness, and an absent-mindedness that made me think to myself, "What's the matter with me?" While it did not actually occur to me that something was wrong with my health, I did have those strange feelings. So that, during the past two years, though I was not aware of it, the cancer gradually was spreading to the liver and affecting it.

However, I have never held a fearsome image of cancer as a kind of evil little demon prowling around inside my body, eating it away. Come to think of it, my organs have worked long and hard for me. For a person who was never very robust right from childhood, my inner organs have served me well through extremely strenuous activities. I feel as if I owe them an apology for paying no attention to them for so long. So the old autonomic nervous system worked might and main for me, but when the balance went out of kilter, it was like Rover taking good-natured bites at my hand. So I love my body, cancer and all. It has worked well for me up to now, and I have no morbid sense of fear. And here and now I have a very cheerful and peaceful feeling as I carry on my life in hospital,but—well—it looks from a common sense standpoint as if my life on this earth is more or less at an end.

Actually, you know, thinking about these two years I mentioned give me a rather good feeling, and I'll tell you why. You might well say, "Frankly speaking, you've been careless about your health. Surely you ought to have paid more attention sooner;" and I'd have to beat myself over the head. However two years ago was just the time when the Kyodan was issuing its declaration of war guilt, and I was the person immediately responsible. A violent controversy arose.

If at that time I had been a person who took excessive care of his own health, I think that, in view of my unusual physical condition, I would have had a thorough physical examination, found that I had a trace of cancer of the pancreas, entered hospital immediately and had an extensive operation. In all probability, from then on, I should have become a half functioning person and withdrawn completely from work, and lived to this very day preoccupied with my own health.

But when you stop to think about it, and certainly as far as I am concerned, the two years that have elapsed to this day have been a turning point for the Kyodan, a period when things were happening. With the declaration of war guilt as a central issue, the Kyodan has taken a stand of independence and justice, clarified her relationship with the Korean church as well as her position with respect to the church in America, and made explicit her basic Christian attitude. She has, moreover, stated plainly her feelings about the Vietnam war, and, for the first time extended the hand of friendship, not only to the churches of the west, but to those of the east through my presence as moderator at the peace congress in Prague. Furthermore, as a concrete expression of our confession of responsibility in the war, we united, as you all know, with the Church of Christ in Okinawa, now called Okinawa Kyoku, and as another expression of this acceptance of responsibility, we established a committee for Christians to work positively on behalf of the South and North Koreans living in Japan. As Chairman of this committee I have made efforts in cooperation with South and North Koreans and with Japanese. Among other things, as a special effort of the Kyodan, plans have been pressed forward for the establishment of the Hiroshima Home for Elderly A-bomb Victims. . . .

Suddenly "tomorrow" became non-existent. When there is no "tomorrow," your "today" also evaporates. A dark feeling came over me that evening, and lasted for about two hours. As I lay there, I felt as if a black cloud was pressing down on my chest. I couldn't bring myself to talk to anyone about it.

The way that Reiko told me about it came about in this way. Dr. Fukumi who is in charge of me, as well as Dr. Ebizawa and others connected with my case apparently knew my condition from the beginning. A number of the elders evidently consulted with one another, deeply anxious about what was best to do, whether to tell me or whether to withhold the information from me until the very end, pastor and all though I was. The upshot was that I ought to be told, and Dr. Fukumi said, "In that case, I'd better tell him." Then, on the other hand it was proposed that another pastor be asked to inform me. Various proposals were made, apparently, but in the end it was deemed advisable that Reiko be the one to tell me. In any case this is how I understand it came about, but Reiko kept quiet about it for several days, talking about various other things, carrying the burden in her heart alone, and suffering deeply, I know. However, finally she broke it to me in a very serene way and for this I am truly thankful. And I am grateful to the doctors and the elders who in the end made this decision after mature deliberation. For I myself was half in doubt about things. I thought to myself, "It's strange for a mere condition of chronic hepatitis to act like this. There's something funny about this, something suspicious." To be sure, they were giving me close attention and thorough medical treatment, but somehow I felt as if there was no clear goal. However, when I heard the true facts, an exceedingly clear goal took shape. My entire life, from its very centre, became extremely clear with a transparently deep meaning. For this I want to thank from the bottom of my heart all those who have lavished such concern on me.

Still, when all's said and done, the night I was told, it came as a shock, coming as it did entirely unexpectedly. And though I was resting in bed, I couldn't settle down; the fact is my nerves were in a highly excited state. I felt as if I was resisting with all my strength the dark thing I spoke of that was pressing down on my chest.

I began to pray in a way I had never done till that moment. It was not just the usual "Heavenly Father," but was like a child, calling to its father: "My father, my father in heaven" *(Ten no otosan, otosan)* I kept saying it over and over, then, "O Christ, O Holy Spirit, O give my spirit strength and bring peace to my heart, and out of the strength and peace that you can give, grant me, even in the midst of this, to sleep soundly till morning."

And so, before long, I went to sleep, and slept restfully until daybreak. And when I awoke, an amazing strength had been instilled into my heart. Since that time, I have not experienced that sense of fear again. On the contrary, everything became clear-cut as I mentioned before, and the brightness has remained. Since then, the strength and brightness that were given to me have never left me for a single day. Since that day I have not felt grief in any radical sense. Thus the shock I spoke of was something that lasted only that evening from the time I got the news until about midnight.

Just the same, however, while I have been feeling basically a sense of cheer in my heart, when an intimate friend came to see me, tears just seemed to flow naturally. Why in the world was it that, even though I wasn't sad, I would break into tears in a way I had never done before?

Of course I thought about my family. In particular the thought of my mother brought me heartache. One after another the members of my congregation and my close friends came rising before my mind. Feeling cheerful and all though I was, I couldn't keep the tears from welling up in my eyes day after day. However, little by little, this changed, and when I see my friends now I do not shed tears, and it might very well be that there are those who think it a bit strange that I do not seem to be sad over parting with them. In any case, there has been a change.

The fact is that I have come to feel, to a depth I never felt before, the power and the reality of God the Father, the Son and the Holy Spirit, and the Kingdom of Heaven. And I have become aware of a certain truth. When I first became ill and took for granted that "Tomorrow" lay ahead, a time when I would return once again to the life of this world, I could feel "Today" as being very much alive. But when "Tomorrow" disappeared, "Today" also disappeared, and a dark feeling came over me. But one evening, when I had Reiko read the Epistle to the Philippians, I heard the words of Paul who, in the face of the imminent death of his physical body, spoke to the Christians with a heart overflowing with joy.

I feel now as if I were feeling for the first time in my life the strength of the life that flows from the Bible. Paul did not regard the moment of his death as the ultimate goal of his life, but rather, transcending that, spoke of the day when he would meet Jesus Christ, the Day of Christ Jesus, as he called it.

It is this that is the real "Tomorrow", a truly shining tomorrow. I have understood this well enough with my mind up to the present, but it is as if I have come to understand it in an absolutely new way. Tomorrow has become truly shining ahead, transcending a mere return to the busy round of this life, transcending death itself; and when this tomorrow became a reality, today became something living before my very eyes as never before.

Thus my way of looking at life has changed in this way: In the last analysis, it isn't a question of acquitting oneself well and being faithful unto death. This is impossible for the very reason that death is a nothing, and a nothing has no future, and you cannot set a nothing before you as a goal and live today meaningfully. Only when the real tomorrow, the day of Christ Jesus, becomes the true future, then and then only does today become filled, for you, with a shining meaning. It is not as though I am living from day to day waiting for death. For example, today is a few days after the end of June, and whatever I have, whether it's cancer or something else, I am living each day meaningfully as a human being living in this world. And tomorrow is also alive for me.

And so, in the days ahead, well, there is such a thing as the death of the body, but I shall walk through the shadow of death, and, in the guiding power of the Lord, surmount it. It is a somewhat unexpected path, but when all is said and done, I shall continue to live, and this I have really come to understand. And since this is the path that the Lord has laid before me, I shall be granted the discovery of a whole new way of life.

When I reached this point in my thinking, I stopped asking myself, "Why, when my heart is not sad, do my tears flow?" A person who came to see me once said just before leaving, "If you're feeling so full of life, you must be all right." I do not agree. When all's said and done, it has nothing to do with whether I am still full of life or not. So, my friends, when you come to see me, it doesn't matter if you say after leaving, "He put on a show of being better than he is; he doesn't seem all that weak," or whether you say, "Buck up." Actually this is beside the point.

Now, with regard to the question whether we go to heaven, up to the present, I have talked about going to be with God, going to be with Christ, going to be with the Holy Spirit as a matter of course, and I could take it for granted for the very reason that it has absolutely nothing to do with my excellency or otherwise. To put it in a crazy way, if the likes of me cannot enter heaven, the very validity of reliance on Christ comes into question, for it is precisely on the Lord's grace and mercy that I depend for everything. And it is the same for all of you. For this very reason I believe from my heart that I shall meet you in the Kingdom of Heaven, and look forward to meeting you once again in the midst of great splendour.

Still and all, while it is only a small matter, when it comes down to actually facing physical death, there is still the lingering thought: How painful it is! But a little while ago I had a dream, or something like one.

A lot of my friends were killed in the war. One of them named Masao Ito was in Manchuria and was killed by a bullet through the head when a Russian tank advanced on him. Another named Ukon Miyanohara died of starvation, after the end of the war, in the mountains in the Philippines. Both of them were fine Christians. (In my dream) these two, Miyanohara and Masao Ito wearing the steel helmet through which the bullet went. The place was a battlefield, but seemed like a meadow in heaven, and both of them, looking really well and fit, were smiling, and looking towards me and saying, "Suzuki-san, there's nothing to worry about." I myself believe now that, when the moment comes for my physical death, I shall take my leave without any worries and in perfect peace.

Well, I have tried to tell you what my mental attitude has been of late. I want you all, my friends, to live to the full, and I want to thank you all. And I would like to add just one more word. In Japan, when it comes to a funeral, it is thought to be quite fitting to shed tears, and this is so for Christians as well. There is a meaning in feeling grief and in shedding tears, but for us to weep and to grieve excessively may well imply that we do not really believe that Christ is the Lord of this world.

MASAHISA SUZUKI

NOTE: The United Church of Christ in Japan is called the Kyodan.

THE TIME MY FATHER DIED

Sometime past noon, November ninth the last, our telephone rang. It was for me, person-to-person. My oldest sister, Margaret, was calling. "Joe, Papa just died!"

We children never called him Papa while we were growing up. He was mostly "Dad." But in the last decade or so, out of a strange mellowing affection, we started, all seven of us, referring to our father as Papa.

My Papa dead!—just seven days before he was ninety-two.

Within the hour I began my journey to my father. I find it difficult to express how deeply I wanted to be with him in his death. Furthermore he had long since commissioned my brother and me to conduct the celebration. My brother unfortunately was out of the country and I had quiet anxiety about executing it alone.

The late afternoon flight was conducive to contemplation. I thought of the many well-meant condolences already received.

"Isn't it fine that your father lived to be ninety-two?"

"It must be easier for you since he lived such a long life."

Certainly I was grateful for such comments. But I found myself perturbed too. Didn't they realize that to die is to die, whether you are seventeen, forty-nine, or one hundred and ten? Didn't they know that our death is our death? And that each of us has only one death to die? This was my father's death! It was no less significant because he was most of a hundred. It was his death. The only one he would ever have.

The family had already gathered when I arrived in the little New England town. We immediately sat in council. The first task was to clarify our self-understanding. The second was to embody that understanding in the celebration of Papa's death. Consensus was already present: the One who gives us our life is the same that takes it from us. From this stance we felt certain broad implications should guide the formation of the ceremony.

> Death is a very lively part of a man's life and no life is finished without the experience of death.

> Death is a crucial point in the human adventure which somehow transposes to every other aspect of life.

> Death is to be received in humble gratitude and must ever be honored with honest dignity.

Together we concluded that the death of our father must be celebrated as a real part of his history, before the final Author that gave him both his life and his death, with integrity and solemn appreciation.

The very articulation of these lines of guidance worked backward laying bare our own inward flight from death. They also made more obvious the efforts of our culture to disguise death. I mean the great concealment by means of plush caskets, white satin linings, soft cushions, head pillows, Sunday clothes, cosmetics, perfume, flowers, and guaranteed vaults. Empty of symbolic meaning, they serve but to deceive—to simulate life. They seem to say, Nothing has actually happened, Nothing is really changed. What vanity to denude death! All our pretenses about it only strengthen its power to destroy our lives. Death stripped of meaning and dignity becomes a demon. Not to embrace death as part of our given life is finally not to embrace our life. That is, we do not really live. This is the power of unacknowledged death. I ponder over the strange smile on faces of the dead.

.　.　.　.　.　.　.　.　.　.　.

"What we all seem to want nowadays," the undertaker said, "is to get rid of the body as quickly and efficiently as is respectably allowable, with as little trouble to as few folk as possible."

These solemn words were creatively sobering. The funeral embodied the full office of worship. We who gathered acted out all three parts. We first confessed our own self-illusions and received once again the word of cosmic promise of fresh beginnings. Then we read to ourselves from our classic scriptures recounting men's courage to be before God and boldly expressed together our thanksgiving for the given actualities of our lives. Thirdly, we presented ourselves to the Unchanging Mystery beyond all that is and corporately dedicated our lives once more to the task of affirming the world and creating civilization.

The point is, we did not gather to console ourselves. We did not gather to psychologically bolster one another. We did not gather to excuse anybody's existence or to pretend about the world we live in. We celebrated the death of my father by recollecting and acknowledging who we are and what we must therefore become. That is, we assembled as the Church on this occasion in our history, to remember that we are the Church.

In the midst of the service of death the "words over the dead" are pronounced. I had sensed for a long time that one day I might pronounce them over Papa. Now that the time had come I found myself melancholy beyond due. It was not simply that it was my father. Yet just because it was my father, I was perhaps acutely sensitive. I mean about the funeral meditation, as it is revealingly termed. Memories of poetic rationalizations of our human pretenses about death gnawed at my spirit. Some that I recalled actually seemed designed to blanket the awareness that comes in the face of death, that death is a part of life and that all must die. I remembered others as attempts to explain away the sharp sense of ontological guilt and moral emptiness that we all experience before the dead. The very gifts of grace were here denied, whether by ignorance or intent, and the human spirit thereby smothered into nothing. I remembered still other of these meditations even more grotesque in their disfigurement of life—undisguised sentimentalities offering shallow assurances and fanciful comforts. How could we shepherds of the souls of men do such things to human beings? Perhaps after all, I was not unduly depressed.

Coincidental with these broodings, my imagination was vividly assaulted by another image. It was a homely scene from a television western. A small crowd of townfolk were assembled on Boot Hill to pay last respects to one who had lived and died outside the law. A very ordinary citizen was asked to say "a-few-words-over-the-dead." He spoke with the plainness of wisdom born out of intimate living with life as it actually is. Protesting that he was not a religious man, he reminded the gathered of the mystery present in that situation beyond the understanding of any one or all of them together. Then he turned and spoke words to the dead one. He spoke words to the family. He spoke words to the townsfolk themselves. In each case his words confronted the intended hearer with the real events and guilt of the past and in each case he offered an image of significance for the future. There was comfort in his words. But it was the honest, painful comfort of coming to terms with who we are in the midst of the world as it is. It impressed me as deeply religious, as deeply Christian. For my father, I took this pattern as my own.

At the appointed place I, too, reminded the assembled

body of the Incomprehensible One who is the ground of all living and dying. I, too, announced a word to the assembled townsfolk, and to my family, and to my father.

I looked out at the members of the funeral party who represented the village where my father had spent his last years. They were sitting face to face before one another, each caught in the gaze of his neighbor. In that moment, if I had never known it before, I knew that a community's life is somehow held before it whenever it takes, with even vague seriousness, the death of one of its members. I saw in its face its failures and fears, its acts of injustice, callousness, and irresponsibility. I saw its guilt. I saw its despair. They would call it sorrow for a passing one. But it was their sorrow. Indeed it was, in a strange way, sorrow for themselves.

In the name of the Church, I spoke, first, of all this which they already knew yet so desperately needed to know aloud. And then I pronounced all their past, remembered and forgotten, fully and finally received before the Unconditioned Being who is Lord both of life and death.

I looked out at my family. There was my mother surrounded by her children and her children's children. What was going on in the deeps of this woman who had mixed her destiny with that of the dead man for the major share of a century? What of sister Margaret who knew so well the severity of her father? What of the son who had never won approval? Or the son-in-law never quite received. What of the one who knew hidden things? What of the rebellious one? What of the specially favored? What of Alice? What of Arthur? What of Elizabeth? I knew, as I looked, perhaps all over again, that the sorrow at death is not only that of the loss of the cherished and the familiar. It is the sorrow of unacknowledged guilt, postponed intentions, buried animosities, unmended ruptures. The sorrow of the funeral is the pain of our own creatureliness, of self-disclosure, and of self-acknowledgment. It is the pain of turning from the past to the future. It is the pain of having to decide all over again about our lives.

In the name of the Church, I spoke of these things written so clearly upon our family countenance. And then in fear and joy pronounced all our relations with Papa and one another as cosmically approved by the One who gives us our lives and takes them from us once again.

I looked at my father. And I knew things in a way I had not known them before. It wasn't that I knew anything new. But my knowing was now transposed so that everything was different. I knew his very tragic boyhood. I knew the scars it engraved on his soul. I knew his lifelong agonizing struggle to rise beyond them. I knew his unknown greatness. I knew his qualities next to genius that never found deliverance. I knew his secret sense of failure. I knew things he never knew I knew. I knew the dark nights of his soul. I knew, well, what I knew was his life. His spirit's journey. That was it. It was his life I knew in that moment. It was frozen now. It was all in now. It was complete. It was finished. It was offered up for what it was. This was the difference made by death.

In the name of the Church, I spoke his life out loud. Not excusing, not glorifying, just of his life as I saw it then. And then I pronounced it good and great and utterly significant before the One who had given it to history just as it was. Not as it might have been, not as it could have been abstractly considered, not as I might have wanted it to be or others felt it should have been, not even as Papa might have wanted it altered. I sealed it as acceptable to God, then just as it was finished.

JOSEPH W. MATHEWS

THE FALSE SELF

The "false self" must not be identified with the body. The body is neither evil nor unreal. It has a reality that is given it by God, and this reality is therefore holy. Hence we say rightly, though symbolically, that the body is the "temple of God," meaning that His truth, His perfect reality, is enshrined there in the mystery of our own being. Let no one, then, dare to hate or to despise the body that has been entrusted to him by God, and let no one dare to misuse this body. Let him not desecrate his own natural unity by dividing himself, soul against body, as if the soul were good and the body evil. Soul and body together subsist in the reality of the hidden, inner person. If the two are separated from one another, there is no longer a person, there is no longer a living, subsisting reality made in the image and likeness of God. The "marriage" of body and soul in one person is one of the things that makes man the image of God ; and what God has joined no man can separate without danger to his sanity.

It is equally false to treat the soul as if it were the "whole self" and the body as if it were the "whole self." Those who make the first mistake fall into the sin of angelism. Those who make the second live below the level assigned by God to human nature. (It would be an easy cliché to say they live like beasts; but this is not always true, by any means.) There are many respectable and even conventionally moral people for whom there is no other reality in life than their body and its relationship with "things." They have reduced themselves to a life lived within the limits of their five senses. Their self is consequently an illusion based on sense experience and nothing else. For these the body becomes a source of falsity and deception; but that is not the body's fault. It is the fault of the person himself, who consents to the illusion, who finds security in self-deception and will not answer the secret voice of God calling him to take a risk and venture by faith outside the reassuring and protective limits of his five senses.

THOMAS MERTON

THE ZENITH OF LIFE

Alfred Schmidt-Sas, a teacher and musician, born March 26, 1895, dedicated himself as an educator and agitator to the struggle against the National Socialist movement. He suffered imprisonment in concentration camps several times over. On October 9, 1942, he was condemned to death by the People's Court; he was executed in Plötzensee on April 9, 1943.

136

A deep, liberating peace encircles me. An astounding emotion wells up in me and fills me wholly: the essential element in life and in man is not affected by death. And so I remain completely with you, and you with me. I die with an exaltation that does not tolerate even tears—just think, not even tears. I stand face to face with the world in inexpressible purity, stand at its center, and these last hours are in truth the zenith of life—the zenith of life.

What I still have to write now is of only two kinds—words of thanks, and words of my never-ending love for you. My imperfect verses are a weak reflection of things you originally gave me. In the measure in which I have become increasingly aware of your love (while it in turn has grown to the point of surrender of your life), in the measure in which I have learned to love you, to love you ever more deeply, in that measure I have become perfect, in that measure the bright glow of kindness has spread wider, the confusion of the world has cleared away, strength and happiness have grown within me, and I have become well-disposed toward all men and have loved our earth anew: this, my dearest, has been your handiwork. And there was a merciful dispensation in your last visit, our last sense-perceptible union; had we known the future, we might not have had strength enough. So I see you present to me as a picture of most beatific hope, and I die as though I were clinging to your lips in a kiss.

I cannot speak to you of my love; it has become so strong that it bursts asunder all forms of speech.

My plea is: Do not close yourself to the beauty of this world, surrender yourself to life; through your being, your art, through your voice, create joy, happiness, kindness, and peace. How much I should like to help you in that. Let all who have helped in shaping me know that these final hours and this death are the crowning of my life, and

that I remain completely yours

O strange luminous life so close to death

Almost nine paces long
Is this my final whitened world.

Still nine days more, perhaps—
Then will fall
My head,
Which now still thinks and speaks and sees and hears.

The great sleep hovers very near,
With its dark pinion overshadowing
The blinding fire of wishes and of fears.
It mitigates the bitter, anguishful,
The longest moments of this human pain.

O strangely luminous life so close to death.*

ALFRED SCHMIDT-SAS

*Written with manacled hands.

UNEARNED SUFFERING

Due to my involvement in the struggle for the freedom of my
people, I have known very few quiet days in the last few
years. I have been arrested five times and put in Alabama
jails. My home has been bombed twice. A day seldom passes
that my family and I are not the recipients of threats of death.
    . . . Recognizing the necessity for suffering I have tried
to make of it a virtue. If only to save myself from bitterness,
I have attempted to see my personal ordeals as an opportunity to transform myself and heal the people involved in
the tragic situation which now obtains. I have lived these
last few years with the conviction that unearned suffering is
redemptive.

MARTIN LUTHER KING, JR.

ON SUFFERING

It is not true that "God tries those whom he loves." But it is
true that the more we suffer, the more Christ is present in

138

us. Because he has already suffered and conquered our suffering, he is aware of us and available to us—not to remove our suffering, but to allow us to conquer it in turn, through his love, and to turn it into a redemptive force.

As long as a child plays quietly, his mother remains in the kitchen preparing dinner. But if he does something naughty and hurts himself, his screams will bring the mother running to help him. Despite his behavior, she is there, more attentive and loving than ever. But the child, nonetheless, can rebel against his hurt. He can throw himself on the floor; he can kick the piece of furniture on which he hurt himself; he can strike out at his mother who is trying to help him. In that case, he suffers even more, for his pain remains and he now has to bear it alone—along with his frustration. But if he loves his mother, he goes beyond his pain and throws himself into her arms. She does not take away the hurt, but, in holding her child, she bears his hurt with him.

In the same way, suffering can either separate us from God or bring us closer to him. Man can reject Jesus, who is present within that suffering. He can accuse Jesus of causing the pain and try to "get even" with Jesus. Or, having heard Jesus softly speak his invitation to love, he can, by assenting with all his strength to Jesus' redemptive act, abandon himself to the Savior, and offer himself by allowing himself to be offered. In that sense, where there is much sin, there Jesus is most present in order to receive and pardon. Where there is much suffering, Jesus is most present in order to save his child; that is, to love him.

MICHEL QUOIST

OUR FATHER'S ADDRESS

It seems to be true today, in a more tragic sense than perhaps it was true in the past, that men are not merely prodigal from their Father's home but have actually forgotten the Father's address. Some seem to have forgotten even that they have a Father. Christ came to announce the fact of the Father, to reveal the Father's love and to be the Father's saving grace to men. He came to us in the far country. He paid the price of seeking us out there. He found us and shamed us out of our sin. He assured us of our Father's love and welcome. He led us home.

To us whose experience this is, belongs the privilege and responsibility of announcing the fact and the act of God in Christ. It is our task to make the Father's address known, to be signposts directing travelers to the Father's presence, to be guides showing the way to the Father's home.

How can we accomplish this task? How can we help men to see that Jesus is the true Shepherd of their lives, and that it is through him they can enter into life's fullness? How can we help them to make the Christ-God discovery?

They cannot begin with God, since to ask God is to ask for the unknown: and yet they do begin with God since this search for God is the cry of the soul for home, and that cry is man's starting point. Men do not know whom they are looking for but, when they find Him, they will be able to recognize Him. That is the paradox of the religious search, and it is as Jesus fulfills this paradox that men know that he is God.

God is the ground of being, so that it is meaningless to speak about proving the existence of God. It is not possible to get outside God in such a way as to make Him an object of proof. What is possible and what is necessary is to come to rest consciously in Him. The "anxiety" which haunts the human spirit is the best security against its coming to rest anywhere except in God. "Our souls are restless until they rest in Him."

D.T. NILES

CHOOSE ANEW

Every day, we must choose ourselves anew; every day, we must choose our lives anew—that is, the people who are around us, the places where we are, the things in which we participate. All of that life must become ours; for that life is the "daily bread" that we must assimilate into ourselves.

At the same time, we must offer it to Christ, who asks for it. We must allow Christ to transform it within himself and assimilate it totally so that—with our help—he may actualize the mystery of his Incarnation. For man's free and loving "yes" to his present life is the key to the mystical Incarnation of Jesus which lies at the heart of creation.

Certainly, not every life can be taken by Christ unto himself. It must be a life which is spent according to the will of the Father; that is, a life spent in the betterment of man and in the building-up of the world. That which goes against the will of the Father—that which is sin—is rejected automatically, like an anti-body, for it can provide no nourishment to the Body of Christ.

Man is saved by his life; not the life that he would like to live, or the life that he dreams of living, but the life that he lives from day to day. Indeed, outside of life, there is no salvation.

MICHEL QUOIST

AN ORDINARY AND COMMON EXPERIENCE

My state of mind, when it became apparent that the therapy had failed and that the practical options open to me were limited and, in each case, both disagreeable and dangerous, was informed privately chiefly by the terms with which I had come to deal with the pain—that pain is not something extraordinary or abnormal but the same reality as work, the concrete experience of fallenness—and by my understanding of the vocational character of decision. It was a state of mind freed, in this way, from potential hang-ups of all sorts. That is to say, I knew that there was nothing traumatic, nothing heroic, nothing tragic, nothing stoic, nothing dramatic in my situation. In truth, mine was a commonplace experience, not only in relation to the circumstances of other human beings, but also in relation to my own history. I realized I had to make some decision, but it was as if I had already rehearsed that decision one million times whenever I had theretofore made any decision about anything. Moreover,

I knew that it did not matter what my decision would be vo-
cationally. The decision might well affect how long I sur-
vived, it certainly would affect the physiology of my survival,
but neither of these matters altered the vocational issue,
which is to live as a human being while one lives. Nor did
survival, for whatever time and in whatever health, change
the moral significance of my decision, since that pertains
to God's own judgment, about which I could only confess
ignorance, together with a confidence in His mercy.

With this outlook, the decision was made, and quite mat-
ter-of-factly, without excitement, lucidly, unanxious about
any future, almost casually. I would have surgery.

I felt like a human being. I felt free.

WILLIAM STRINGFELLOW

ONE CONQUERS DEATH BY LOVE

To live inauthentically in the world, to spend one's whole
life evading the reality of death, and then, on top of all that,
to tell oneself that one has the answer to the question of
what happens after death: this can be a further depth of
self-deception. One can perhaps succeed in this by a naive
and stubborn insistence on believing that after death everything will continue to be just as it is now: except that care
and pain will not be problems any longer. Such an attitude
is not Christian, it is simply a regression to a crass form of
paganism. The Christian faith does not give us detailed and
precise answers as to what happens after death: but it does
urge us to face death, and take it into account, and overcome our fear of it, and conquer it in Christ. That is quite
another matter.

More Christians ought to realize this, instead of making
their pious considerations of heaven and hell (if any) simply
a way of evading the need to face death in its reality. But,
once again, the Christian faith does not seek merely to an-

swer the question "What comes after death?" Rather it answers the question we ask about death itself: what is death? What does death mean, in my own existence now? For death is not merely the inevitable *end* of life, an end that must come whether one likes it or not. It is not merely a painful necessity, like paying income tax. The fact of death is not merely the closing of all possibilities, the negation of choice and hope. I am not free not to die, but I remain free to make what I like out of a life that must end in death. But an authentic use of this freedom demands that I take death into account. To pretend to live as if I could not be touched by death is not a rational and human use of freedom. Such "freedom" is actually without any meaning at all. It is a delusion.

At the heart of the Christian faith is the conviction that, when death is accepted in a spirit of faith, and when one's whole life is oriented to self-giving so that at its end one gladly and freely surrenders it back into the hands of God the Creator and Redeemer, then death is transformed into a fulfillment. One conquers death by love—not by one's own heroic virtuousness, but by sharing in that love with which Christ accepted death on the Cross. This is not apparent to reason: it is, precisely, a matter of faith. But the Christian is one who believes that when he has united his life and his death with Christ's gift of Himself on the Cross, he has not merely found a dogmatic answer to a human problem and a set of ritual gestures which comfort and allay anxiety: he has gained access to the grace of the Holy Spirit. Therefore he lives no longer by his own forfeited and fallen existence, but by the eternal and immortal life that is given him, in the Spirit, by Christ. He lives "in Christ."

What then "comes after death" is still not made clear in terms of a "place of rest" (a celestial cemetery?) or a paradise of reward. The Christian is not concerned really with a life divided between this world and the next. He is concerned with one life, the new life of man (Adam—all men) in Christ and in the Spirit, both now and after death. He does not ask for a blueprint of his heavenly mansion. He seeks the Face of God, and the vision of Him Who is eternal life. (John 17:3)

THOMAS MERTON

AN ECUMENICAL SACRAMENT

I had all the time there is; the time had come for the Eucharist. The first hospital night had passed without pain, though I had not taken medication which had been supplied. I slept soundly, though I had not used the sleeping tablets that were prescribed, having a prejudice against their use, which I attribute to my Yankee inheritance. Anthony had arrived in the city that evening and had come to Columbia-Presbyterian to see that I was settled. He had come bearing various messages and several gifts.

The featured present was a circus poster, which he hung in the room so that it would be a constant vision no matter how I might be positioned. He knew this would comfort and delight me, since I am a more than avid fan of the circus, regarding it as the auspices of the most sophisticated and versatile performing arts and counting the survival of the circus in America as a reliable gauge of the survival of civility itself. I am, of course, referring to the circus—not to Disney productions, not to Ed Sullivan's facsimiles, not to the Broadway pretenses with which John Ringling North, as if renouncing his birthright, had adulterated the arena performances of "The Greatest Show on Earth"—where it retains integrity both as art and enterprise. In the summer of 1966, Anthony and I had spent nearly three months traveling with the Clyde Beatty-Cole Brothers Circus, the largest remaining tented show, in order to gather material and gain first-hand background for a book I purpose to write about the idea of society as a circus and, hence, the circus as an eschatological scene. Roughly half of that book had been written when I became enough impaired by the disease that it had to be put aside until a more opportune time. It was a gift which suited the circumstances entirely.

As if to multiply my pleasure, I opened one of the messages that Anthony brought to find a note from Corita Kent —who had become celebrated as Sister Corita of the Order of the Immaculate Heart of Mary for her serigraphs and whom I had asked to do the jacket for my circus book— together with one of her posters announcing an edition of her work under the legend (a citation from e. e. cummings) "damn everything but the circus."

During the next morning I had received telephone calls from Giselle Klopstock and the Rev. Melvin Schoonover. Giselle had indicated that she or Robert would visit sometime that day. Mel and I had been friends and colleagues since 1956 in East Harlem. He had been administrator of the East Harlem Protestant Parish, but had resigned from the group ministry, not long after I had done the same, and subsequently became minister of the Chambers Memorial Baptist Church in the same neighborhood. I had been his best man in his wedding and his daughter, Polly, was one of my godchildren, whom I regularly took to the circus, of course. Mel has been unable to walk since his birth and functions with impressive agility and virtual independence from his wheel chair. He knows more of illness and pain and, therefore, more about health and wholeness, than any other person within my experience. Though he is consistently cool about his own condition, I detected, in our conversation on the phone, that he was anxious about my condition, and I had sought to change the subject by asking his suggestions for a Christmas present for Polly.

Thomas Pike, a priest from the city, deeply involved through the Episcopal Peace Fellowship in the anti-war protests (recently he was arrested, with others, for praying on Pentagon premises), had also been in touch with me at the hospital, particularly to ask if I wished to receive the Holy Communion. Tom said he would be there to assist Bishop Wetmore.

Early in the afternoon, Anthony returned to the hospital and he and I talked about the circus, as if to anticipate the Eucharist.

Soon Dan Berrigan joined us, then Mel Schoonover, Robert Klopstock, Tom Pike. By the arrival of the bishop, Ann Thompson and Merritt Hedgeman had also appeared. Ann Thompson is an earnest and gifted Christian whom Anthony and I had come to know when we shared a household in the city. She had been our housekeeper, and she had brought some order to our home, but, more than that, she is a radiant person, and she had brought some light there too. We had kept in touch with her after immigrating to the Island. Anthony had written to her about my situation. Together with his wife, Anna Arnold Hedgeman, an illustrious pioneer among black women in America, Merritt Hedgeman had been staunch counsel for years in the vicissitudes that I, as a white man, had to confront on the scene of the black revolt.

Those who had not met before were introduced by Anthony and, as that happened, it seemed to me that my biography was being recited, so truly did this congregation conjoin to represent many persons and many things that I had known and for which I cared. More important, it was a *good* congregation in which there were old and young, rich and poor, white and black; in which Anglicans, Baptists, Roman Catholics, Pentecostals, Methodists, and lapsed churchmen were present: in which some had education, but some not, some had known imprisonments, but some had not, some were of the establishment, but some not.

Bishop Wetmore declared the sacrament of Holy Communion is ecumenical and that everyone would be welcome to receive the bread and the wine. He asked Father Berrigan to read the Epistle. And so, together, thanksgiving for life was made to God.

Afterward, as people dispersed, Anthony escorted the bishop to the elevator. When he came back to the room, and after we were alone, he said that as they walked down the hall, Bishop Wetmore had remarked, with evident excitement: "What an extraordinary congregation that was! I wish they were all like that!"

WILLIAM STRINGFELLOW

ULTIMATE WISDOM

The way Mrs. —— bears her pains and awaits her ultimate and certain dissolution with childlike faith and inner serenity is an achievement which philosophers might well envy. I declare that there is a quality in the lives of unschooled people, if they have made good use of the school of life and pain, which wins my admiration much more than anything you can find in effete circles. There is less of that whining rebellion against life's fortunes, less morbid introspection and more faith in the goodness of God. And that faith is, whatever the little cynics may say, really ultimate wisdom.

Mrs. —— has had a hard life, raised a large family under great difficulties, is revered by her children, respected by her friends, and she has learned to view the difficult future with quiet courage as she surveys the painful and yet happy past with sincere gratitude. She thanks me for praying with her and imagines that I am doing her a favor to come to see her. But I really come for selfish reasons—because I leave that home with a more radiant faith of my own. My confidence in both man and God is strengthened.

It is the quality in that woman's life that seems to me to be dissipated in the modern day, for all our progress. Perhaps we will work out something comparable to it some day in a highly disciplined culture. But as we lose the moral fibre of the generation of pioneers and wait for the discipline of a generation of moral aristocracy, it is ordained that we should wander through this present world where life is too comfortable to have the tragic nobility which our fathers had and too chaotic to disclose the charms which come from a great cultural and moral tradition.

REINHOLD NIEBUHR

HOW DO YOU WANT TO DIE?

There are two ways to ask the question, "How would you like to die?" The obvious answer: "If I have a choice, I should prefer not at all." There is too much fun in being alive to think about death; so why ask the question?

There is another way to ask the question, "How would you like to die?" If we accent the how, then we have some choice. We may smoke ourselves to death. A medical friend of mine has suggested that I should remind our students that if they want a $16,000 death, the most horrible kind of all, then keep on smoking. Or we may drink ourselves to death. Lots of deaths begin at the cocktail hour.

Whether or not we have an answer to the question, it is certain that we know how we would not like to die. We do not want to die in a flaming wreck on the highway. We would avoid violent death in a riot. We prefer not a long period of helpless wasting away, dying a little at a time. All of us would much prefer a quick and easy way. That is, when work is done we lay down the tools of our trade and sleep on into the future life.

But another thing has brought this theme home to me: my own experience. Until the fall of 1969 I had had unusually good health. I had been an athlete; outdoor life was a joy; even minor aches and pains were minimal, considering that I was more than twice past the over-30 age. And then suddenly it came. It came with that frightful word, "malignancy!" I have spent long hours alone in meditation, and in the early days of the experience there was a smothering sense that I was sure to die. The only question was, "How soon?" What would happen in the meantime?

This gave me time to reflect upon memories. Reaching back into the years, I picked up incidents and experiences which had seemed very precious. Then I remembered the tasks yet to be done, papers to be written, classes to be met, sermons to be preached, a little black book full of engagements, and the thought of that cemetery lot with my wife's name and mine on the marker.

During this time of meditation I had a talk with God about death. I had written about death and philosophized about it a good bit, but now I faced it. I told God here were four things that I could do. I reminded God that I could die; and I honestly said to Him that if this were best, I would not rebel. I suggested that I would be happy to be healed. I believe in Divine healing, and if this would be my privilege, I should be grateful. The third thing was that I would be willing to live under a handicap, to accept a crippled condition of life, provided I had His help. But I reminded God there was one thing I was not willing to do, and this was to endure this illness alone, with my own strength.

It was interesting that in the midst of these meditations, there should come to me the impulse to prepare a sermon on the subject, *How would you like to die?* Now Paul in the fourth chapter of Second Corinthians has two very interesting statements. He says, "We have this treasure in earthen vessels." How true that is. Earthen vessels are so easily broken. He also says, "Our outer nature is wasting away; our inner nature is being renewed every day." And how true that is. The body disintegrates. It has been accurately said that our death begins the day we are born. But also there is the assurance that our inner nature can be renewed every day. This is faith.

I have come to feel that life is measured in terms of death — not the other way around. The late William E. Hocking of Harvard University once wrote a book on *Thoughts on Death and Life*. Normally we should write it "thoughts on life and death," but not Professor Hocking. He, too, saw that life is measured in the light of death — and this is our theme.

What does it all mean?

1) I have come to feel, in facing this question of the growing importance of each day, the New Testament emphasis upon today. There is a kind of warning not to harden our hearts today. This is the urgency of the now time. A young minister came into my office and told me how he was listening to Billy Graham on the television when Billy Graham made the statement, "This is the hour of decision." Then he added, "And this was my hour." The now time was surrender to Jesus Christ.

This means that whatever we have to do, we have only a minute of time in which to do it. That means we must assess the value of each day and thank God for each day as that day comes. We understand what the man meant when he said, "So much to do, so little time to do it." I have a friend, a great prayer leader, who closes each day with an interesting prayer. He reminds God that he returns his life to God each evening to commit it to God's care for the night. He tells God also that if he awakens to receive it back the next day to live it, he is grateful. But if it is God's will for Him to take it, then he is committed.

The question is: What are we going to do with each of these days? You see, there is a delicate significance with each day. We sing, "Lord for tomorrow and its needs I do not pray; Keep me, my God, from stain of sin/Just for today." This is the importance of daily things. It reminds us of the inescapability of death, that we are not skillful enough to manage our lives even for one day. It is so easy to foul up our lines and get the job of life all mixed up until life is tangled; we cannot unsnarl it.

2) Then, in the second place, this matter of how I should like to die is very personal. It has brought my wife and me much closer together in our own fellowship. Perhaps one reason for this is that we have experienced the uncertainty of many homes. One of the tragedies which have touched our lives has been the breakdown of families that have been close friends of ours. And even when it seems necessary or inevitable, it still carries with it a sadness.

Death has helped my wife and me to face our own weaknesses and to live a life of love beyond the places where we have failed. We, too, have discovered that our home is an earthen vessel. I think we understand better now the struggles of others and have a deeper sympathy for them; we can feel the hurt of other families as they fail.

Again, the prayer time has been much more meaningful in our family. We remember that we do not know how many more mornings we may have together. We have experienced the joy of helping some of our children and their families plan a trip to the Orient. We actually have counted the days before they were to leave. And then we reflected upon our own trip around the world, and we counted the days prior to departure. But in our prayer time we count differently. We count each day as precious.

This means that we have tried to make our home more of a center of concern for other people. For several years now we have had a prayer breakfast in our home. We meet at a quarter of seven for a simple finger breakfast and then have about 35 minutes for prayer time. Students from other countries have been with us; faculty members have come. We have tried to make this a time of community intercession in behalf of people in need. This has brought us not only closer to each other but to our students.

And then again, this has brought us joy in simple things. In the face of death true happiness is not seen as being amused by things on the outside; that is, to be entertained is not primarily our concern. The TV mentality of our time when we have to be constantly amused has lost any significance it may have had. We watch the birds in the feeder outside our window. We see the joy of little children as they play in the yard. We experience the thrill of a quiet sail on the lake. We read together some great piece of literature. There is joy in simple things.

And so, as Paul would say, while we have this treasure in earthen vessels, there are some treasures which are not of earthen vessels. And just as our outer nature is wasting away, there is the inner nature which is being renewed day by day. This grows.

3) In the face of death we are reminded of our debt to others. And this has created a growing concern for other people. We have come to feel that we are bound together until we belong to one another. No man is an island. We have responsibilities that reach beyond our own family. So when we talk about having a treasure in earthen vessels, we are reminded that we are all in it together.

This came home to me with vividness while I was in the hospital. There I watched the skilled hands and brains of trained surgeons. I felt the tenderness of nurses as they sought to minister. I experienced the thoughtfulness of students, faculty, and friends as they came to see me. And so in the midst of mortality, I turned again to see how much other people really mean to me.

In the midst of this I began to reflect upon three men whose lives have made the greatest contribution to my own life. One was my father, a man who had limited opportunities but who sacrificed that I might have the best opportunities. Another was my great professor, Edwin Lewis, whose mind and insight have been matched by no man I have ever met. He, too, contributed greatly to me. And the third is still with us, though now well in his years. I refer to E. Stanley Jones,* whose devotion and worldwide witness have lifted my own soul time and time again. It has been a privilege to work very intimately with Brother Stanley in the Ashram Fellowship and in other places.

And then I think of a blasted world. I see the news on television, and I see films of Viet Nam and remember the privilege my wife and I had of walking in the refugee villages there and seeing the wrecked homes of people, the broken lives and ask, "How long, O God, how long?"

*E. Stanley Jones died in India, January, 1973. Ed.

I recall walking in the streets of Calcutta at night when one had to be careful not to step upon the masses of people sleeping on the streets since they had nowhere else to sleep. I see the refugees in the village of Quang Ngai in Viet Nam. I can visualize the H-block houses in Hong Kong, and I've been in the rat holes of Atlanta where people exist, not live. I am trying to say that when one looks death in the face he stands with multitudes in our world today. He knows that life is very precarious. We begin to see that life is not measured in terms of the abundance of the things that we possess.

One of the things my wife and I have done is to go through things which have cluttered and accumulated in our home. We have tried to rid ourselves of "things," the accumulations that we do not need. And then I see a TV picture of refugees, often these people carrying the total possessions they have on a bag on their back.

You see, this calls us to invest in the lives of others while we are still alive. My wife and I stood in Saigon and saw a triple amputee being given a wheelchair in which he could move around the hospital. There were 2,400 Vietnamese soldiers in that hospital. The simple thing of a wheelchair which could be bought for about $100 brought such joy to the face of this young man that it moved us greatly.

Then I think of a man by the name of Kawabe, who built a church, a hostel, a clinic, at the edge of Expo '70 in Osaka, when he talked to us about the privilege of this hostel housing students from the university when Expo was over. My wife and I felt constrained to invest in it and help furnish a room for these students. Then only recently, just before Expo opened, we received a letter from Mrs. Kawabe, that great little soul who loved so deeply, who established prayer groups all over the country of Japan, whose own evangelical witness moved the hearts and lives of people. Her letter said he had died just before he saw the hostel opened. A growing concern for others, this has come to us in the light of death.

4) I have come to see that the growth of a Christian faith must be anchored not in the past but in the future. I think of the life of Jesus; it was cut off so early. Then I think of my own life. I am already nearly twice as old as he was when he died. And he loved life, wanted it, cried out against death,

and yet accepted it when he saw that it meant redemption for the lives of others.

You see, I am trying to say that Christian faith is not merely rooted in the past. Yes, of course, it is rooted in what Christ did and what he said and what he provided. He made once for all the sacrifice for the sins of the whole world. Yet the Christian faith is also anchored in the future. At the present time there is much emphasis on what is known as a "theology of hope" calling us into the tomorrows. The God of the Christian is not only the God of the past and the present, but he is also the God of the future. The idea of promise of things yet to be burns deeply in the hearts and lives of the Christian.

So you see, there are really two outlooks on life which are influencing our time. One is the talk about the good old days. It is the attempt to live in yesterday. We have memories of how wonderful things were. I have a suspicion they were not quite so wonderful as we sometimes think. But it is a view of looking back. It is back to the Bible, back to the New Testament, back to the old-time religion.

I remember visiting a medical doctor once when he asked the question, "When are we ever going to get back to the good old days?" He was somewhat surprised by my answer when I said, "Thank God, we are never going back to the good old days!" I paused a little while to let what I had said burn into his mind and then added, "That is not the way we are going. Any good old days we have are going to have to be from now on out."

Another outlook on life is the existentialist point of view that places the emphasis on now. It often has no sense of history on the one hand and no hope for tomorrow. It accents the glorious present moment. One man has defined existentialism in this fashion: "I and Thou,/Here and now,/Wow!"

But there is a third way, another outlook on life. It is the certainty that whatever tomorrow brings, the future will be under the direction of God. This determines the way we live, not simply what has gone, not simply what is now, but in terms of what shall be. This is not the idea of the other worldliness of Christianity as sometimes we are criticized for holding, but it is the certainty that tomorrow belongs to God.

Thus I am coming to see there must be a theology of death.

The most certain fact about life is death; it pushes into life whether we want it or not. For the death of the individual is necessary for the perpetuation of the race. It is unthinkable that we should be born into a world, live in that world without death ever coming. God's plan is for the many to live awhile, then die and make room for others, rather than for a few to be permanent here. Of course, all our efforts to prolong life I know never end even in a hospital where I have received such excellent attention and where I am quite willing to go when it is necessary. But I remember that even in the hospital all the attempts to keep life going fail in the end.

Of course, it is possible for life to lose its meaning for ourselves, but we can never be so callous as to have life lose its meaning for others. Death is judgment. It brings judgment in the shortness of time. The finality of time is that it discloses the weakness of our own self-sufficiency. There is both a democracy and an injustice in life which is dramatized by death.

Thus, I have come to feel that death is a sacrament, that there is a divine pain in death in which God's final appeal is in terms of the Cross. This is the suffering of the God of the Christian. The Christian God bears an agony at the very center of his personal life. As one man put it, "There was a cross on the heart of God before there was a cross on the hill of Calvary." This means that death itself becomes God's final appeal to man. When we come to the end of our abilities, it is a reminder that God still has something to say.

Thus, we come to our question, "How would you like to die?" May I suggest one of the most glorious things of death. The New Testament has a curious and vivid emphasis. It is death to the old way of life, to the old habits, to the old values, to the old pleasures, to the old person, the old style of life. "If any man be in Christ he is a new creation, old things are passed away, behold they have become new." And Paul dramatically set it forth when he said, "I am crucified with Christ, nevertheless I live." There is a death to the inner life which is sub-Christian. There is a crucifixion of the self in which the things which we treasure so much pass away and the eternal values of the God of the open tomb become real.

Well, how would you like to die? Remember, Paul says we have this treasure in earthen vessels and that applies to all of us. He also says while this outward nature is wasting away the inner nature is being renewed day by day.

I should appeal, therefore, to us all even as I do for myself until the life I live may not be a life measured in terms of the calendar, but in terms of eternity. And so the life that I live today becomes His life which he gives to me now. It is life beyond the reach of death. This is the secret of the Christian's confrontation with that strange experience we call death.

How do you want to die?

CLAUDE H. THOMPSON

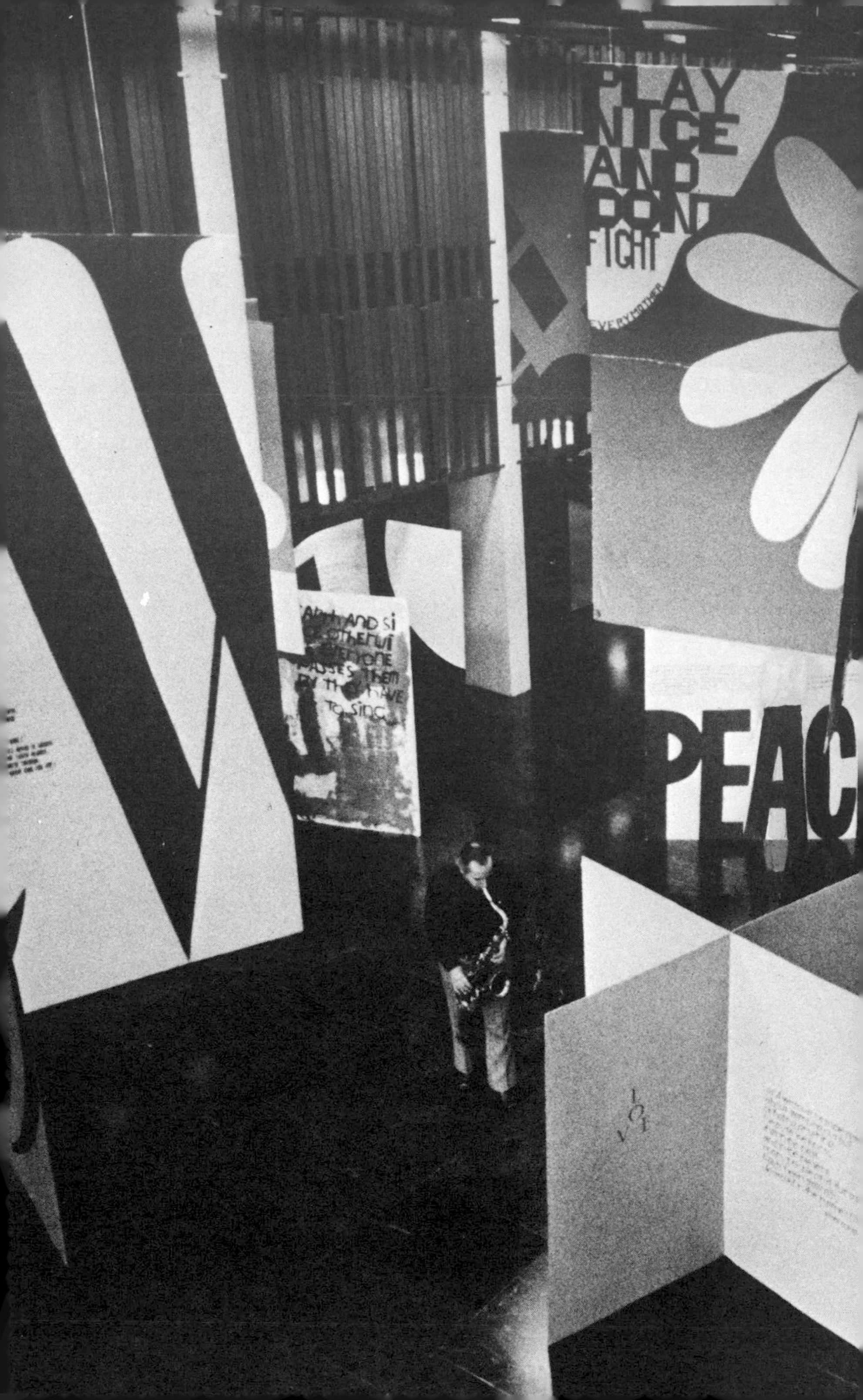
PLAY
NICE
AND
DONT
FIGHT
PEAC

JOY,
FREEDOM, PEACE

5 JOY, FREEDOM, PEACE

JOY, FREEDOM, PEACE

Just as Faith, Hope, and Love cannot be compartmentalized, we think you have already encountered Joy, Freedom, and Peace in this book. It could be argued that they are interchangeable. Surely all these fruits of the Spirit are found among the Witnesses, in the Church and World, in our Life and Death. But we have chosen to end this book on a note of celebration and these things seem eminently celebratory. So our troops are gathered again to lead us in celebration. One thing about Christian celebration. It isn't done very well alone. It is done in company of others, in our rites and rituals, our songs and prayers, our all too occasional shouts and hallelujahs. We have added to our celebration a theologian of play, Harvey Cox. He began by looking at the problems of the secular city and ended up at "the feast of fools." Father Clarence Joseph Rivers is a black priest whose original worship services and music have brought him public acclaim. His two books, *Reflections* and *Celebration* delight in worshiping God in a contemporary manner. We live in a time when the celebration of God's goodness is being experienced in many different ways, reaching back to early worship and ahead to the music and words of tomorrow. Celebration looks back in gratitude, recalling what God has done for us and is doing today and looks forward in hope and joy.

ON JOY

Joy is prayer—Joy is strength—Joy is love—Joy is the net of love by which you can catch souls. God loves a cheerful giver. She gives most who gives with joy. The best way to show our gratitude to God and the people is to accept everything with joy. A joyful heart is the normal result of a heart burning with love. Never let anything so fill you with sorrow as to make you forget the joy of Christ Risen.

We all long for heaven where God is, but we have it in our power to be in heaven with him right now—to be happy with him at this very moment. But being happy with him now means:

> loving as he loves,
> helping as he helps,
> giving as he gives,
> serving as he serves,
> rescuing as he rescues,
> being with him twenty-four hours,
> touching him in his distressing disguise.

MOTHER TERESA

EVERY MOMENT JOY

If we are willing, every moment of our lives can resound with the joy of Easter. And the true Christian cannot live without joy. Through Christ, he encounters joy and lives in joy. He is given over to joy. In his life there can be no enduring failure—neither suffering nor death are insurmountable obstacles for him. Everything is the raw material of redemption, of resurrection, for, in the middle of his sufferings and his deaths, Christ the Conqueror waits. If a Christian is unhappy, it can only be because he has succumbed to the temptation to flirt with death and to turn his back on life. For that reason, the greatest suffering and the greatest joy can coexist in the same life and be intimately interconnected to one another. By "joy" we do not mean the transient (though legitimate) pleasure that comes from comfort, or the false happiness of the simple mind that is unaware of his degradation, or the "virtuous" resignation of a pseudo-mystic, or the blind optimism of the man who figures that "it is better to laugh than to cry." We mean rather the calm, the interior serenity, and the profound peace which permeate and emanate from a man who, notwithstanding a torn heart and body, and despite the suffering of mankind and the world, believes with all his strength in the victory of the Savior. And he believes this without for an instant forgetting or denying the existence of suffering and sin, and without giving up the fight against them.

MICHEL QUOIST

FREEDOM TO BREATHE

A shower fell in the night and now dark clouds drift across the sky, occasionally sprinkling a fine film of rain.

I stand under an apple tree in blossom and I breathe. Not only the apple tree but the grass round it glistens with moisture; words cannot describe the sweet fragrance that pervades the air. I inhale as deeply as I can, and the aroma invades my whole being; I breathe with my eyes open, I breathe with my eyes closed—I cannot say which gives me the greater pleasure.

This, I believe, is the single most precious freedom that prison takes away from us; the freedom to breathe freely, as I now can. No food on earth, no wine, not even a woman's kiss is sweeter to me than this air steeped in the fragrance of flowers, of moisture and freshness.

No matter that this is only a tiny garden, hemmed in by five-story houses like cages in a zoo. I cease to hear the motorcycles backfiring, radios whining, the burble of loudspeakers. As long as there is fresh air to breathe under an apple tree after a shower, we may survive a little longer.

ALEXANDER SOLZHENITSYN

SHOUT WITH JOY

I must say to each of you that I have made my decision.

I'm reminded of a story. Centuries ago King Nebuchadnezzar issued an order to all who fell under his domain. That order was that at the sound of the trumpet everyone was to bow before the golden image. The refusal to bow would mean that one would be thrown into the fiery furnace. There were three young men who heard the order. They knew of the injunction, but something deep within them told them that they had to violate the injunction and practice civil disobedience. They stood before the king and said: "We know that the God that we worship is able to deliver us . . . but if not, we will not bow. We know that the power that we have experienced and read about in nature is able to deliver us. We know that the force who has the power to throw up the giant mountains, kissing the skies as if to bathe their peaks in the lofty blue, the power to throw out the stars to bedeck the heavens like swinging lanterns of eternity, also has the power to deliver us . . . but if not, we will not bow." They were saying that they had discovered something so dear, so precious and so great that they were going to live with it. They had come to say that they were going to do what conscience told them was right. They discovered that ultimately a great faith is not a bargaining faith. It is never an "if" faith, but it is a "though" faith. It doesn't say, if you do this for me, God, if you do this on that point and that on the other point, then I will serve you; but it goes on to say, "Though he slay me, yet I will trust him." And the great experiences of life are "though" experiences. Marriage is never a bargaining experience, it's a though experience.

I've decided that, on this question of non-violence, I'm going to stand by it. I'm going to love because it's just lovely to love. I'm going to be non-violent because I believe it is the answer to mankind's problems. I'm not going to bargain with reality, but I'm going to stand by non-violence in spite of. And I say to you that I've taken a vow—I, Martin Luther King, take thee, Non-violence, to be my wedded wife, for better or for worse, for richer or for poorer—this isn't a bargaining experience—for richer or for poorer, in sickness and in health, until death do us part. I'm going on in the faith, and with that determination. I believe if we maintain faith and then escalate our actions we will be able to go to Washington and we will be able to create vibrant movement throughout the cities of our country. And by the thousands we will move, and many will wonder where we are coming from, and our only answer will be that we are coming up out of great trials and tribulations. Some of us will come from Mississippi, some of us will come from Alabama, some from Chicago, some from Detroit, some from Cleveland, but we will all be coming from the same condition. We will be seeking a city whose builder and maker is God. And if we will do this, we will be able to turn this nation upside down and right side up, and we may just be able to speed up the day when men everywhere will be able to cry out that we are children of God, made in his image. This will be a glorious day; at that moment the morning stars will sing together, and sons of God will shout for joy.

MARTIN LUTHER KING, JR.

LIBERTY

And because men have often made a bad use of what they called their 'liberty', we see today those who are tempted to renounce this liberty; the success of dictatorship in politics is simply due to the fact that people are so tired of the effort to rule themselves that they willingly hand over their responsibilities to someone who is stronger than they are. And because dictators are almost always people who believe in no one save themselves; who depend on their own strength and their own wisdom, they can only maintain their regime by force. 'If God does not exist, then everything is permitted.' This famous saying from a hero in one of Dostoevsky's works has been cruelly verified in history in men like Hitler and Stalin.

Where God does not reign, man finishes by regarding himself as a god. The demon of power holds him in its grip.

We live in a time when some people are clamouring passionately for liberty, while others ignore it because they are disillusioned.

In both cases two things have been forgotten: first of all, that liberty is never an end in itself. We are liberated from something and for something. The true question is this: 'From what do you want to be liberated? and for what?'

Secondly, exterior liberty—political or material—is nothing without an interior liberty; it can only lead to new forms of slavery.

SUZANNE de DIETRICH

SORROW AND JOY

Sorrow and joy,
striking suddenly on our startled senses,
seem, at the first approach, all but impossible
of just distinction one from the other,
even as frost and heat at the first keen contact
burn us alike.

Joy and sorrow,
hurled from the height of heaven in meteor fashion,
flash in an arc of shining menace o'er us.
Those they touch are left
stricken amid the fragments
of their colourless, usual lives.

Imperturbable, mighty,
ruinous and compelling,
sorrow and joy
—summoned or all unsought for—
processionally enter.
Those they encounter
they transfigure, investing them
with strange gravity
and a spirit of worship.

Joy is rich in fears;
sorrow has its sweetness.

Indistinguishable from each other
they approach us from eternity,
equally potent in their power and terror.

From every quarter
mortals come hurrying,
part envious, part awe-struck
swarming, and peering
into the portent,
where the mystery sent from above us
is transmuting into the inevitable
order of earthly human drama.

What, then, is joy? What, then, is sorrow?
Time alone can decide between them,
when the immediate poignant happening
lengthens out to continuous wearisome suffering
when the laboured creeping moments of daylight
slowly uncover the fullness of our disaster,
sorrow's unmistakable features.

Then do most of our kind,
sated, if only by the monotony
of unrelieved unhappiness,
turn away from the drama, disillusioned,
uncompassionate.

O ye mothers and loved ones—then, ah, then
comes your hour, the hour for true devotion.
Then your hour comes, ye friends and brothers!
Loyal hearts can change the face of sorrow,
softly encircle it with love's most gentle
unearthly radiance.

DIETRICH BONHOEFFER

PURE JOY

(The following letter was written by Daniel Berrigan to his mother, to his brother Jerome and sister-in-law Carol, and other members of his family.)

Danbury [Prison]
Oct. 12, 1970, Mon. p.m.
Dear Ones.

What you do for us here, heads & hearts! It was as usual a very pure kind of joy—and bracing too, when we saw you on the hillside. Then the children run down like healers in their own right! I was literally shocked to see how they had grown; mostly the changes in their faces, something I find beyond prediction. One grows so used to the faces of old-sters and tends to equate children's bones in somewhat a settled way. Well, they are more beautiful than ever—and so are yez, with your lamps within.

.   .   .   .

I suspect this is going to be a rich sort of year for all of us. When events so conspired, I tried to tell myself I saw so many priests sliding down the play yard on their pants into middle age. All major decisions made—nothing but a shabby decency at the end. And suddenly a great light shone —on us. Not that we saw it, but we believed. There was go-ing to be a chance of second birth in middle age—an utterly new form of life, placed in other hands; a kind of second chance; out of which something might emerge for others, in a harried, bewildered time. Here we are. Even a prom-ised land, if we can recognize the promise.

You were "into" this as you had been in everything. I almost said, a part of this—except that spiritual realities have nothing to do with parts and portions. You were wholly in this with the wholeness which love both demands & confers —whole loaf, multiplied, for all. This is I think a clue to the special joy, the "terrible beauty" which is born in our faces when we meet & part. When we scan each other, as though our faces were a topography of the weather of the heart— what is being born, what is dying, what we can bear together.

Then one thinks of our brothers and sisters across the world (especially of others here) and knows that on the com-mon scale of mankind, we are being asked to bear only what good men and women are bearing everywhere—and much less than most. But enough, for suffering, for acceptance.

DANIEL BERRIGAN

TRUE JOY

The only true joy on earth is to escape from the prison of our own false self, and enter by love into union with the Life Who dwells and sings within the essence of every creature and in the core of our own souls. In His love we possess all things and enjoy fruition of them, finding Him in them all. And thus as we go about the world, everything we meet and everything we see and hear and touch, far from defiling, purifies us and plants in us something more of contemplation and of heaven.

Short of this perfection, created things do not bring us joy but pain. Until we love God perfectly, everything in the world will be able to hurt us. And the greatest misfortune is to be dead to the pain they inflict on us, and not to realize what it is.

THOMAS MERTON

A MATTER OF EXPRESSION

Without ritual man loses his sense of transcendence. But through ritual man becomes gravity-free.

Life does have its kicks; but some of its kicks can land "where it hurts." Life hurts when one cannot see, cannot foresee, any fruit to one's efforts. When there is no proof that life has meaning, one could at least hope that it does. Without hope one loses faith in life's promise. When the world seems set against what it might be, when the unchained forces of nature and the armed forces of nations are aligned against "well-being," one can at least hope that ultimately the thrust behind the world is a benign one. If man cannot hope, he lives in despair. He may not commit physical suicide, but his life in despair is suicidal, lifeless. To despair of life is to live in death.

The primary source of faith and hope, the sources most evident to us, are the lives of people around us. When we experience "care" of others for us, it is easier for us to believe and to hope in the Ultimate Caring of the universe. If we experience the love of our fellow men, it is much easier to believe that "God is love." When we see others struggling against impossible odds and triumphing (albeit only occasionally) we are led to hope that ultimately the forces of "good" will overcome.

Now although life itself is our first and most important teacher, life experience as expressed in art forms can teach us what we might have missed in raw life or what we might not have been able to survive. Life experience brought to us in the art of celebration can rescue when life itself affords no hope. It is therefore necessary that we keep all kinds of celebrations alive, whether we identify them as religious or secular.

Man's problems in this world derive at least partially from the simple fact that he is less than God. When he is born into this world he knows nothing, but even when he has gained in knowledge and wisdom to his ultimate capacity —man is still less than all-knowing and therefore in spite of all the light at his disposal, is still surrounded by a certain (frequently fearsome) darkness. When he is born into this world he is capable of little—indefensible, highly impregnable; but then when he has gained in power to his ultimate capacity—man is still less than all-powerful, still less than all-mighty; and therefore in spite of all his might, he is at some point a prey to a frustrating helplessness. After he has surrounded himself with the sturdiest walls and the widest moats of defense that his wisdom and power will allow, man finds that something is beyond his control, capable of penetrating his defenses. And he must live with the unsettling thought that he, like Achilles, has a pregnable, defenseless heel, that his plans can miscarry and that he himself can be destroyed.

Frequently terrified by what he does not know, greatly frustrated by what he cannot accomplish, man has a desperate need of some assurance, however vague, that life is really worthwhile, has ultimate meaning. He needs a witness to the fact that there is a concerned wisdom, and a caring power in the universe. If you will, he must be assured that there is a living God—who knows his plight, who cares, and who is capable of overcoming—whom man can trust to see where man himself cannot see and whom man can trust to do what man himself cannot do. Without this witness, man is open to despair. Without this witness God is dead for most men. And neither the words and arguments of theologians nor the pronouncements of bishops and popes, are sufficient to bring him to life—unless they are accompanied by living witness. Indeed if there is living witness, the pronouncements will become unnecessary.

CLARENCE JOSEPH RIVERS

ON PLAY

What is serious to men is often very trivial in the sight of God. What in God might appear to us as "play" is perhaps what He Himself takes most seriously. At any rate the Lord plays and diverts Himself in the garden of His creation, and if we could let go of our own obsession with what we think is the meaning of it all, we might be able to hear His call and follow Him in His mysterious, cosmic dance. We do not have to go very far to catch echoes of that game, and of that dancing. When we are alone on a starlight night; when by chance we see the migrating birds in autumn descending on a grove of junipers to rest and eat; when we see children in a moment when they are really children; when we know love in our own hearts; or, when, like the Japanese poet Bashó we hear an old frog land in a quiet pond with a solitary splash—at such times the awakening, the turning inside out of all values, the "newness," the emptiness and the purity of vision that make themselves evident, provide a glimpse of the cosmic dance.

For the world and time are the dance of the Lord in emptiness. The silence of the spheres is the music of a wedding feast. The more we persist in misunderstanding the phenomena of life, the more we analyze them out into strange finalities and complex purposes of our own, the more we involve ourselves in sadness, absurdity and despair. But it does not matter much, because no despair of ours can alter the reality of things, or stain the joy of the cosmic dance which is always there. Indeed, we are in the midst of it, and it is in the midst of us, for it beats in our very blood, whether we want it to or not.

Yet the fact remains that we are invited to forget ourselves on purpose, cast our awful solemnity to the winds and join in the general dance.

THOMAS MERTON

OUTSIDE MY WINDOW

Outside my window
Noisy voices rise
Shouting my name;
    And I,
(Would-be philosopher,
Apostle thinly clad),
Within my den
Raise up my head,
And look to see
    Who calls.

Is it a human mother
    Suckling there
Her clock-faced boy
With filthy nose.
Or are they animals
Far, far removed from man?
The glass distorts them . . . .
There a little girl
    Frolics about,
    Face painted
With a fierce moustache . . . .

A baby toddles by . . . .
The bell upon a dog's neck
    Tinkles . . . .
Tiny new-hatched
Chickens cheep . . . .

Cast-off clogs,

And broken sandals,
And foul, reeking mud
Make one great compost-heap . . . .
  Everywhere
I know that vile things
Jump, and crawl, and leap . . . .

    Chatter, chatter;
    Peep, peep;
    Clatter, clatter;
    Mumble, tumble;
    Grumble, rumble;
    Growl, yowl, howl . . . .

    And over all
    The hot rays
    Of the sun
    Beat on the slum
    Like some
    Great drum . . . .

This is no time
    Nor place
For cold philosophy.

Come, little black-nosed babe,
Come fierce moustache,
    Come dog,
Come dirty chicks,
We shall join hands,
    And prance,
    And dance,
    And dance . . . .

                    TOYOHIKO KAGAWA

THE REALITY BEHIND THE DANCE

Birth and death, love and pain—the reality behind the dance
under the daylight lamps of social responsibility.

How well I understand the mirror symbolism in Cocteau's *Orphée*. To break through the barrier which, when I encounter reality, prevents my encountering myself—to break through it, even at the price of having to enter the Kingdom of Death. Nevertheless—what do I long for more ardently than just this? When and how shall I find the occasion to do it? Or is it already too late?

Is my contact with others anything more than a contact with reflections? Who or what can give me the power to transform the mirror into a doorway?

Chance? Necessity? Am I not too "sensible and well-balanced," that is to say, too self-centered socially to surrender to anything less than a necessity? One which can be accounted for!

"At the frontier of the unheard-of—" Aware of the consummation of the deep-sea dive—but afraid, by instinct, experience, education, for "certain reasons," of putting my head under water, ignorant, even, of how it is done.

The stream of life through millions of years, the stream of human lives through countless centuries. Evil, death and dearth, sacrifice and love—what does "I" mean in such a perspective? Reason tells me that I am bound to seek my own good, seek to gratify my desires, win power for myself and admiration from others. And yet I "know"—know without knowing—that, in such a perspective, nothing could be less important. A vision in which God is.

DAG HAMMARSKJÖLD

BARTH'S DREAM

Karl Barth had a dream about Mozart.

Barth had always been piqued by the Catholicism of Mozart, and by Mozart's rejection of Protestantism. For Mozart said that "Protestantism was all in the head" and that "Protestants did not know the meaning of the *Agnus Dei qui tollis peccata mundi*."

Barth, in his dream, was appointed to examine Mozart in theology. He wanted to make the examination as favorable as possible, and in his questions he alluded pointedly to Mozart's masses.

But Mozart did not answer a word.

I was deeply moved by Barth's account of this dream and almost wanted to write him a letter about it. The dream concerns his salvation, and Barth perhaps is striving to admit that he will be saved more by the Mozart in himself than by his theology.

Each day, for years, Barth played Mozart every morning before going to work on his dogma; unconsciously seeking to awaken, perhaps, the hidden sophianic Mozart in himself, the central wisdom that comes in tune with the divine and cosmic music and is saved by love, yes, even by *eros.* While the other, theological self, seemingly more concerned with love, grasps at a more stern, more cerebral *agape;* a love that, after all, is not in our own heart but *only in God* and revealed only to our head.

Barth says, also significantly, that "it is a child, even a 'divine' child, who speaks in Mozart's music to us." Some, he says, considered Mozart always a child in practical affairs (but Burckhardt "earnestly took exception" to this view). At the same time, Mozart, the child prodigy, "was never allowed to be a child in the literal meaning of that word." He gave his first concert at the age of six.

Yet he was always a child "in the higher meaning of that word."

Fear not, Karl Barth! Trust in the divine mercy. Though you have grown up to become a theologian, Christ remains a child in you. Your books (and mine) matter less than we might think! There is in us a Mozart who will be our salvation.

THOMAS MERTON

I DO NOT LOOK BACK

We have seen what the liberty of Jesus Christ means; we have seen that Satan has no power over him; we have seen that his will was wholly one with that of the Father, that his heart beat in union with the Father's heart; we have seen him giving his life freely for his brethren.

It is this liberty which he wants to communicate to us; it is this liberty which he wants to live within us.

'Hereby know we love, because he laid down his life for us: and we ought to lay down our lives for the brethren.'[1]

We know very well that we do not suddenly pass from the bondage of the old Adam which is selfish, proud, self-centered to that glorious liberty which is that of Christ.

We shall only know the fullness of his love and of his freedom in the world to come. But we count on him; we look up to him; in him, by faith, we have the earnest of this future liberty. And if we allow his Spirit to act within us he does transform us 'into his likeness', we discover more and more even we, that 'where the Spirit of the Lord is, there is liberty'.[2]

What does this mean, in practice—for my daily life?

It means that I commit the past with its sins, its failures or successes to the Lord; that I am no longer the slave of my past; that I do not look back.

This means that I can live fully in the present moment; taste and enjoy all human joys as a gift which God gives to me, and endure all the sufferings and conflicts, because my Lord bears them with me.

This means that I can look forward to 'tomorrow' without anxiety and without panic, for the Lord knows this unknown future; he has prepared it; and he will go through it with me.

Thus he communicates to me his own liberty, with regard to people, things, and circumstances. In him is given back to me the world with all the possibilities, all the riches, which the Creator has placed within it.

The liberty of the Christian allows him to enjoy without scruple, and indeed with fresh intensity, all that the world offers that is beautiful and good.

But it also means that we are to use the things of this world as though they were not[3]—that is to say, we can do without them when they are denied to us; for our real treasure is elsewhere.

That is the joyful liberty which the Lord wills to give even in this life to his own.

SUZANNE de DIETRICH

1. I John 3:16.   2. II Cor. 3.   3. I Cor. 7:31

LAUGHTER REIGNS IN HEAVEN

The laughter of the universe in heaven? Of course. In hell there is no hope and no laughter, according to Dante. In purgatory there is no laughter, but there is hope. In heaven, hope is no longer necessary and laughter reigns.

Comic hope is the mood of our embryonic religious sensibility today. It has left behind orthodox credulity, existential pathos, and sanguine optimism. It supplies the only possible idiom for theology. The new theologians are right that hope is the characteristic form of faith for modern man. But our hope is neither the serene confidence of medieval man, nor the liberal's bright expectation of better things around the corner. Ours is a more or less formless hope, but a hope nonetheless. It is a hope in search of content, a hope that some form of hope will once again be made available to us.

.　.　.　.　.　.　.　.　.　.　.

Laughter is hope's last weapon. Crowded on all sides with idiocy and ugliness, pushed to concede that the final apocalypse seems to be upon us, we seem nonetheless to nourish laughter as our only remaining defense. In the presence of disaster and death we laugh instead of crossing ourselves. Or perhaps better stated, our laughter is our way of crossing ourselves. It shows that despite the disappearance of any empirical basis for hope, we have not stopped hoping. As R. W. B. Lewis says, our sense of the awful nearness of catastrophe lies close to the heart of the imagination today. But it does not paralyze the heart itself. At the very heart of man there lies "a humane perspective rooted not quite in hope but in a hope about hope."

This sense of irrepressible radical hope remains alive and well, in the comic. Its Christ is the painted jester whose foolishness is wiser than wisdom. Its church meets wherever men lift festive bowls to toast joys remembered or anticipated. Its liturgy is the exuberant enactment of fantasy before the eyes of a prosaic world. Its God is the often unspoken ground for refusing to be cowed into timidity or resignation by mere facts.

This gift of comic hope is not something on which religious people hold a monopoly. They share it with all sorts and conditions of men. But it may be the special responsibility of men of faith to nourish this gift, to celebrate this sense of comic hope, and to demonstrate it. It could conceivably disappear, and where laughter and hope have disappeared man has ceased to be man.

HARVEY COX

MERCY AS WELL AS JUDGMENT

There are no simple congruities in life or history. The cult of happiness erroneously assumes them. It is possible to soften the incongruities of life endlessly by the scientific conquest of nature's caprices, and the social and political triumph over historic injustice. But all such strategies cannot finally overcome the fragmentary character of human existence. The final wisdom of life requires, not the annulment of incongruity but the achievement of serenity within and above it.

Nothing that is worth doing can be achieved in our lifetime; therefore we must be saved by hope. Nothing which is true or beautiful or good makes complete sense in any immediate context of history; therefore we must be saved by faith. Nothing we do, however virtuous, can be accomplished alone; therefore we are saved by love. No virtuous act is quite as virtuous from the standpoint of our friend or foe as it is from our standpoint. Therefore we must be saved by the final form of love which is forgiveness.

The irony of America's quest for happiness lies in the fact that she succeeded more obviously than any other nation in making life "comfortable," only finally to run into larger incongruities of human destiny by the same achievements by which it escaped the smaller ones. Thus we tried too simply to make sense out of life, striving for harmonies between man and nature and man and society and man and his ultimate destiny, which have provisional but no ultimate validity. Our very success in this enterprise has hastened the exposure of its final limits. Over these exertions we discern by faith the ironical laughter of the divine source and end of all things. "He that sitteth in the heavens shall

176

laugh" (Psalms 2:4). He laughs because "the people imagine a vain thing." The scripture assures us that God's laughter is derisive, having the sting of judgment upon our vanities in it. But if the laughter is truly ironic it must symbolize mercy as well as judgment. For whenever judgment defines the limits of human striving it creates the possibility of an humble acceptance of those limits. Within that humility mercy and peace find a lodging place.

REINHOLD NIEBUHR

GREAT LAUGHTER

I happen to believe in God because here and there over the years certain things happened. No one particularly untoward thing happened, just certain things. To be more accurate, the things that happened never really were quite certain and hence, I suppose, their queer power.

At twenty-seven, living alone in New York trying with no success to start a novel and in love with a girl who was not in love with me, I went to hear a famous preacher preach one morning although I had no idea at the time that he was famous and went only on impulse—I was not a churchgoer —because his church was next door. It was around the time that Elizabeth II was crowned at Westminster Abbey, and the preacher played variations on the theme of coronation. All I remember of what he said is the very last, and that not well, just one phrase of it, in fact, that I'm sure of. He said that Jesus Christ refused a crown when Satan offered it in the wilderness, or something like that. He said that the kingdom of Jesus was not of this world. And yet again and again, he said, Jesus was crowned in the hearts of those who believed in him, crowned king. I remember thinking that was a nice enough image, as images in sermons go, and I remember how the preacher looked up there in the pulpit twitching around a good deal, it seemed to me, and plucking at the lapels of his black gown. And then he went on just a few sentences more.

He said that unlike Elizabeth's coronation in the Abbey,

this coronation of Jesus in the believer's heart took place among confession—and I thought, yes, yes, confession—and tears, he said—and I thought tears, yes, perfectly plausible that the coronation of Jesus in the believing hearts should take place among confession and tears. And then with his head bobbing up and down so that his glasses glittered, he said in his odd, sandy voice, the voice of an old nurse, that the coronation of Jesus took place among confession and tears and then, as God was and is my witness, *great laughter,* he said. Jesus is crowned among confession and tears and great laughter, and at the phrase *great laughter,* for reasons that I have never satisfactorily understood, the great wall of China crumbled and Atlantis rose up out of the sea, and on Madison Avenue, at 73rd Street, tears leapt from my eyes as though I had been struck across the face.

FREDERICK BUECHNER

A QUESTION OF INTEGRITY

. . . We find in Scripture that there is *no way of serving or loving God directly. We must serve him by serving our fellow man.* Every attempt to serve God merely by so-called religious practices is condemned again and again by the prophets. What words did Isaiah put in the mouth of God: "I don't want your sacrifices, the smell of your incense sickens me, and I am tired of that jangling noise that you call singing . . . but lift the burden from the oppressed, plead the widow's cause, care for the orphan, shelter the homeless, and then come to me. And though your sins be as scarlet, I will wash them whiter than snow."

Jesus said much the same thing: "If anything separates you from your brother, go first and be reconciled to him, and only then will your gift be acceptable at the altar."

The Christian theology of the Incarnation says that Jesus is completely God and completely man. He apparently did not have to become less godly to become thoroughly human, so why should we have to become less human in order to be more godly?

Nevertheless, in the midst of tendencies to keep the secular and the sacred separate, there are signs of hope. Men of religion are becoming actively involved in questions of this world, in questions of everyday living, of art and science, peace, civil rights, urban renewal, in the struggles of the farm-workers, and so on. All of these things are visible signs that we in our times are beginning to put the pieces together once more, that we are "getting ourselves together," becoming integral once more.

In our actions, religion and life, spirit and matter, intellect and emotion, heaven and earth, the sacred and the secular, the natural and the supernatural are reconciled once more. Our efforts are real acts of atonement, at-one-ment. Our efforts are indeed sacramental, not only symbolizing but effecting salvation! It is these efforts that we celebrate.

For centuries we have been singing at the dedication of a Church: "How awe-inspiring is this place! This is the very gate of heaven!" Today we sing these words in the rededication of total, integral, human society with all its art and technology. For this world is the very house of God. This is our gate to heaven. "How awe-inspiring is this place!"

CLARENCE JOSEPH RIVERS

FROM THE INCHOATE TO THE EXPRESSIVE

There is nothing wrong with inventing rituals. All rituals were at one time invented by someone. But if man wants to express his deepest feelings to himself and to other men, ritual must have a social dimension. And if man is to be in touch with what others have sensed in the dim past, or if he wants to pass on his experience to the future, the ritual must have a historical dimension as well. Furthermore, even to express his deepest feelings to himself, man needs a ritual, just as he needs a language even to talk to himself. Ritual does for movement what language does for sound, transforms it from

179

the inchoate into the expressive. Therefore an idiosyncratic ritual is ultimately frustrating and self-defeating.

HARVEY COX

PEACE*

We shall make this year a year of Peace in a particular way —to be able to do this we shall try to talk more to God and with God and less with men and to men. Let us preach the peace of Christ like he did. He went about doing good; he did not stop his works of charity because the Pharisees and others hated him or tried to spoil his Father's work. He just went about doing good. Cardinal Newman wrote: 'Help me to spread thy fragrance everywhere I go—let me preach thee without preaching, not by words but by my example— by the catching force; the sympathetic influence of what I do, the evident fullness of the love my heart beats to thee.' Our works of love are nothing but works of peace. Let us do them with greater love and efficiency—each in her own or his own work in daily life; in your home—in your neighbour. It is always the same Christ who says:

I was hungry—not only for good, but for peace that comes from a pure heart.

I was thirsty—not for water, but for peace that satiates the passionate thirst of passion for war.

I was naked—not for clothes, but for that beautiful dignity of men and women for their bodies.

I was homeless—not for a shelter made of bricks, but for a heart that understands, that covers, that loves.

This year let us be this to Christ in our neighbour wherever the Missionaries of Charity and their Co-Workers be. Let us radiate the peace of God and so light his light and extinguish in the world and in the hearts of all men all hatred, and love for power. Let the Missionaries of Charity and the Co-Workers, in every country wherever they are, meet God with a smile—everywhere they go in everyone.

MOTHER TERESA

* Extract from a letter to the Co-Workers.

LIBERATION IS ALL THROUGH LIFE

Thus the work of liberation goes on all through life. 'Work out your own salvation with fear and trembling', says St. Paul again, 'for it is God which worketh in you both to will and to work for his good pleasure'. You are under grace; God in Jesus Christ has done everything for you: that is why: Work![1]

SUZANNE de DIETRICH

1. Phil. 2:12.

THE END OF LIFE

Whenever you take a stand for truth and justice, you are liable to scorn. Often you will be called an impractical idealist or a dangerous radical. Sometimes it might mean going to jail. If such is the case you must honorably grace the jail with your presence. It might even mean physical death. But if physical death is the price that some must pay to free their children from a permanent life of psychological death, then nothing could be more Christian.

I still believe that standing up for the truth of God is the greatest thing in the world. This is the end of life. The end of life is not to be happy. The end of life is not to achieve pleasure and avoid pain. The end of life is to do the will of God, come what may.

MARTIN LUTHER KING, JR.

CELEBRATION

Underneath, in darkness there was DEATH,
an ever-wasting emptiness,
an overwhelming nothingness,
a world negating void.

But chancing, risking, gambler-like,
LIFE cast into the void the seed of LIFE,

risking loss that gain might come,
burying seed in DEATH.

And then the LIFE in light
called forth the seed from DEATH:
then (alleluia!) sprouting up,
a life to LIFE responded
struggled up—
up against
the world negating void,
cell-by-cell growth,
leaf-by-leaf growth,
toward the call of LIFE in light,
back toward resurrection!

DEATH, then, is nothing all-at-once;
in fact, it always was
all around us always by us,
overwhelming;
myriad its forms.

DEATH is not what we're going to;
DEATH is what we're growing from:
slavery and violence,
the needed song not sung,
the wound unhealed,
the love withheld,
the wonder undiscovered.

Everything that man should be,
yet has not ever been;
everything that man should do,
yet has not ever done;
every wrong instead of right,
every negative — partakes of DEATH,
is part of that relentless void,
that emptiness through which we grow
to reach the light of LIFE.

And therefore resurrection
is never all-at-once;
for we rise up day by day,

cell-by-cell growth,
leaf- by-leaf growth,
toward the light:

A child is born! and we grow!
Lives rebuilding after the ruin!
War is questioned (if not banished)!
Up we grow! Up we grow!
Now a poem! Sanitation! A skyscraper!
Up we grow!
Universal brotherhood, striving to be practiced!
There new nations! Here a new drug!
Tel-star sight and sound!
Up we grow! Growing, growing,
cell-by-cell growth,
leaf- by-leaf growth,
toward th light of resurrection!

CELEBRATE THE FEAST OF LIFE!!!
HE IS RISEN!!! WE ARE RISING!!!
ALLELUIA!!! ALLELUIA!!!

CLARENCE JOSEPH RIVERS

A BABY IS BORN

It is January 9, 1941, and *The New York Times* this morning is filled with news of total war and total defense. Every day four-column headlines of the costs of war: "1942 Budget $17,485,528,049. Funds for British to Be Sought Later."

Wonder what that $49 tacked on the end of the $17,485,-528,000 is for? Fifty dollars, we know, will pay for a baby, if you are poor, at any hospital in the city. A flat rate of fifty dollars, ward care, the ministrations of any doctor that happens to be on hand, and ten days' hospitalization.

At Bellevue Hospital, if you are poor, if you are a resident of the great City of New York, it doesn't cost a cent.

William, our new baby down here at Mott Street, is hereby headlined on our front page, as the biggest news of the month, the gayest news, the most beautiful news, the most tragic news, and indeed more worthy of a place in a headline than the seventenn billion, four hundred and eighty-five million, five hundred and twenty-eight thousand and forty-nine dollars headlined in *The New York Times* this morning. William himself is worth more than that sum, more indeed than all the money in the world. He is indeed but dust, the Lord knoweth it, but he is also little less than the angels. He is a creature of body and soul, a son of God and (by his baptism down at Transfiguration Church last Sunday at 2 p.m.) a temple of the Holy Ghost. For his sake our Lord God came down from Heaven, was begotten by the Holy Ghost, born of the Virgin Mary, was made man, lived with us for thirty-three years, and suffered and laid down His life. For William's sake as well as for the sake of each one of us.

And this tiny creature who little realizes his dignity as a member of the Mystical Body of Christ, lies upstairs from me now as I write, swaddled in a blanket and reposing in a laundry basket. He is rosy and calm and satisfied, a look of infinite peace and complacency upon that tiny countenance. He little knows what is in the world, what horrors beset us on every side.

We had awaited his arrival, the week before Christmas, breathlessly. Every night before we went to bed we asked the young mother, "How do you feel?" and asked each other (us women on the two top floors of St. Joseph's House on Mott Street), "Is there taxi money?" in case it would be too late to call an ambulance.

And then, one morning at five, I heard rapid footsteps in the room above, the voice of the ambulance interne in the hall, "I'll be waiting downstairs." And I realized that the great moment had arrived.

It was still dark out, but it was indubitably morning. Lights were on in the kitchens of surrounding tenements. Fish peddlers, taxi drivers, truckmen, longshoremen, were up and on their way to work. The business of life was beginning. And I thought, "How cheerful to begin to have a baby at this time of the morning!" Not at 2 a.m., for instance, a dreary time of low vitality, when people sink beneath their woes and courage flags. Five o'clock is a cheerful hour.

184

Down in our little backyard (where we had the Christmas tree this year), down in that cavernous pit with tenements looming five and seven stories up around, we could hear them dragging out the ash cans, bringing in the coffee cans for the line.

.   .   .   .

Not one man, not a dear husband, not a protector on whom she could lean for comfort and strength. There was no Joseph on this winter morning. But there were hundreds of men, silent, waiting and wondering perhaps as they watched the ambulance, whether it was life or death that had called it out.

"This is worse than war," one woman friend said a few days before, contemplating the situation. And we agreed, wondering if anything indeed could be more desperate and sad than a woman left to have her child alone.

There you have the tragedy of the refugee, there you have the misery of homelessness, the uncertainty as to food and clothing and shelter (and this woman had known hunger). And there, too, you have the pain and agony of the flesh. No soldier with his guts spilled out on the battlefield, lying for hours impaled upon barbed wire, suffers physically more than a woman in childbirth. Physically, I say, because does not the soldier in his horror and pain wonder what has brought him to this pass — what is being accomplished by the gigantic agony of war? With the woman the suffering brought forth life. In war, death. And despite shame and fear and uncertainty, as in this case, still there cannot but be joy over a child born into the world.

So it is with joy that we announce the newcomer to our House of Hospitality on Mott Street, knowing that our readers who have suffered with us in the past will be glad to rejoice with us now.

For us most truly this has been a season of happiness. "For unto us a son is born, unto us a child is given." Christ Himself came so truly to us this Christmas Day in this baby boy, just as in the persons of the hungry men. "For inasmuch as ye have done it unto one of the least of these my brethren, ye have done it unto me."

DOROTHY DAY

185

HOW TO
USE THIS BOOK

HOW TO USE THIS BOOK

This book is not the usual type of book for study or meditation. Although it may be useful to have one person as a leader or guide, it may be just as useful to rotate leadership or to have team leadership, even in a small group. This book is to be experienced, thought about, meditated upon, felt. Not all readers will have the same reactions. A wide variety of thoughts and emotions are conveyed in the different readings. The authors have had widely different experiences. Some of the material may at first reading seem dense or opaque. Other passages are as flat and as plain as a piece of bread. Some have the immediacy of everyday experience. Others, you will find, are poetic and provocative.

One of the intentions of the book is to display the relationship between contemplation and action. Most of the authors chosen are twentieth century Christians who have been deeply involved in both the disciplines of prayer, meditation, and Biblical study and in the world around them. Several of the writers have suffered deeply for their faith, even to the point of death. We shall seek the source of their courage to take risks and suffer scorn, and shall probe the significance of their Christian belief. The nature of Christian community and the supportive fellowship of the church are also explored.

But the study is not concerned just with the extraordinary, the heroic, the unusual. Ordinary living requires much courage, and we shall consider how to face our own sin, doubt, despair, loneliness and death, and to help others at crisis times. Readers will discover much about themselves and each other by pondering the meaning of these passages. Therefore, while the material of the five sections can be covered in five sessions, the intention of the book is *revelation* rather than information, *discovery* not mastery.

Readers must understand from the beginning that they should learn and grow at their own rate. They are not asked to agree with or approve everything they read. It might be interesting to note how authors in a given section seem to differ with each other in their understanding of *God* and the *world*.

The focus of the study sessions should be upon the reader's understanding of the passages. This means that certain disciplines of thinking and probing will be called upon as the group studies the writings together. But there is no single right way to interpret a passage. In Bible study, students are sometimes admonished not to let the sharing of spiritual insights distract them from the study of the text itself. Here, however, just such sharing will be the *basis* for the community of contemplation and thoughtful study. Persons will find themselves sharing their own thoughts and beliefs. There well may be deep differences in the group — and validly so! An atmosphere in which all feel free to reveal their own beliefs and doubts, some of which may be hesitantly expressed (and gently received), will be most conducive to "spiritual growth."

Some questions which readers might keep in mind as they read are: Is this an authentic expression of Christian personhood? What in my experience (or my friend's) relates to this? What does the Bible have to say on this subject? Some members of the group might keep a Bible "watch," relating passages to Scripture. Where terms such as "salvation," "reconciliation," "resurrection," "prayer," and "Kingdom" are used, are they used in the way your group understands them? If not, attempt your own definitions, parables, concrete examples, to explain these terms.

YOUR OWN BOOK

Christians of our time are introduced here. Perhaps there are some persons of whom you have never heard. If you were doing such a book yourself, which contemporary Christians would you include? Group members might begin such collections of their own. Who *are* the authentic Christians of *your* time and place? How have persons mediated the love of Christ to you? Have they been writers or doers (describe incidents which would convey their witness to others through acts, letters, ideas)? Share your ideas with the group.

At the same time, keep a *journal* of your thoughts. For some this may be so private a journey of self-discovery you may not wish to share it all with others. Include passages of other writers which appeal to you and might be shared with the group. The *journal* can be a composition book (preferably with hard cover), a loose leaf notebook, ledger, or any other sturdy book with blank pages in which you can record your own thoughts, stories of others, and quotations that appeal to you. Do not hesitate to record your own feelings and reactions, or to tell your own story.

Some schools these days have courses in journal writing or autobiography (the New School for Social Research and the lay education series of the New York Theological Seminary are two). One such course is entitled "Life Stories" in which biographies and autobiographies are studied with the single theme: How Did I Grow Into What I Became? The students taking the course for credit keep their own journals to better understand themselves and their own lives. Thus, the students' lives are illuminated both through their own attempts to express themselves and the perception and candor of other lives they study.

In her book, *Our Many Selves,* Elizabeth O'Connor suggests as a final exercise for persons examining their own lives that they write their autobiographies. Her handbook of self-discovery, which would be useful accompaniment to this book, says:

> Do you know what it means to be chosen? Have you ever thought of yourself as chosen? If you did believe this — if you could overcome all your resistances to the idea — would you live your life differently? What would it do to your concept of yourself? Would you act with more pride or more humility?
>
> Reflecting on your whole life, can you see God acting, preparing you for ministry in this present hour? Write a two- or three-page paper including your response to the above question. Note especially the sufferings that crippled you for ministry and those that enabled you to take your place in the tradition of the suffering servant. "With His stripes we are healed." This is also true for His disciples. Celebration and suffering, to our surprise, are closely related. If we are not acquainted with our own suffering, others will instinctively know it. Our wounds do not even have to be healed. We simply have to be conscious of them. If we have not been wounded, we do not know what it feels like. We cannot say to another, "I understand." It is not out of our perfection that we heal, but out of our acquaintance with pain.[1]

[1] *Our Many Selves* by Elizabeth O'Connor, Harper & Row, New York, 1971, pp. 187-188.

RESEARCHING THE AUTHORS

From the extended bibliography, let the group choose authors on which it wishes to do further research and enlist the aid of the church, the community library, the Service Center and local bookstores in tracking down more material on the particular author. Some of the theologians like Tillich, Niebuhr, and Barth, have written short books of sermons as well as more weighty tomes. The students can also seek out the books which tell about these men's lives and reveal why they seem to speak compellingly to so many Christians. Authors like Martin Luther King were greatly criticized in their lifetime. The group might look to see who are the persons today receiving similar criticism and ask "why?" One author, Daniel Berrigan, was imprisoned for his action in destroying draft files in Cambridge, Maryland. The reader can search his essays and poems to see what drove Berrigan to this extreme action (and the group can discuss whether such criminal actions are ever justified). Dietrich Bonhoeffer was hanged for attempting a plot on Hitler's life during the last months of World War II. Is a Christian ever justified in taking life? What of the extreme pacifist views of Daniel Berrigan as opposed to Bonhoeffer's willingness to take a particular life in order to stop a cruel war? What of other wars?

The suggestions here are not dogmatic but are meant to suggest styles of approach to the material. Each group and each leader will have a different style. Various schemes for investigating further the writing of persons included can be developed. Some will be more difficult than others to discover. Masses of material exist on Bonhoeffer, but little of Florence Allshorn is available, although the excellent biography, *Florence Allshorn,* edited by J. H. Oldham is available, and Malcolm Muggeridge's *Something Beautiful for God,* is the only book to tell us about Mother Teresa.

A possible approach is for each person to read through a section marking the passages which speak most directly to them or are most meaningful. The group can share these as a starting point, and the more difficult passages may become clearer as their individual reactions and responses are expressed.

A SAMPLE SESSION OUTLINE FOR A SMALL GROUP

Essential materials:

> TEXT: *The Healing Fountain* by Betty Thompson
> YOUR OWN BOOK: *The journal of your own thoughts
> and favorite quotations*

1. Share with each other one new insight or one text that really "spoke" to you as you read it, each one taking a turn.
2. What did you find hard to understand? What do you think the writer means?
3. What is your experience of:

> Faith, Hope, Love? (Session I)
> Witness? (Session II)
> Church and World? (Session III)
> Life and Death? (Session IV)
> Joy, Freedom, Peace? (Session V)

4. What meanings do you find as you reflect on these experiences?

ART, WORSHIP, BIBLICAL PERSPECTIVE

Create an arts sub-group to go through the writings seeking a sentence or phrase to be illustrated, one for which they can make a colorful poster or "prayer cards" to bring to class. This group could also search out films that deal with the general topics of the book and report on them or have the group see them together.[1] Some may wish to make slides or photographs.

Another group can locate contemporary songs or make a collection from poetry, novels, and plays, which deal with the theme treated in the book, including them in their *journals* and sharing them with the class. Here younger people in the church and community could be of special help.

A *worship group* can prepare for brief worship services or "Moments of Worship" can take place in the total group, using the text as a resource for theme, texts, meditations, prayers, litanies. This group should be free to "race ahead" and use the other sections of the text if a particular author introduced in the first section appears in later ones as well.

---

1. For suggested films and other audio-visual materials, write to the Audio-Visual Office, Room 1333, Board of Global Ministries, United Methodist Church, 475 Riverside Drive, New York, N.Y. 10027.

Other works by the authors can be quoted to enrich the worship content. Celebration, worship, praise should be a dimension of each session not just a subject studied in the last one.

The special task of the *biblical sub-group* could be a study of the relationship of Scripture to the writings in the section. This group need not be concerned with "proof-texting," but try to introduce the biblical dimensions of great themes like "salvation," "resurrection," "discipleship," etc.

The important thing about the Bible passages chosen is that the believers should act upon their belief. It will not be especially helpful in this study to divide consideration into *reflection* and *action*. Instead, the group could try to see what the consequences of spiritual disciplines can be for daily life both for individuals, and for a Christian community. The study should be focused on the resources of faith for action. Rather than assigning a special group to study what faith means in terms of action and to follow the study in the community and world, the whole class should be concerned and through the study become aware of possibilities.

A COMMON READER

The book's omissions can provide a starting point for further quests. Where are the African and Latin American representatives? Some may wish to bring African writers to the group's attention. Few young people are represented as the emphasis is on some of the spiritual "giants" of the immediate past or present. But young people have much to say in their songs and writing. Search for their witness to share with the group. There are more men than women among the writers; yet women provide the bulk of attendance and interest in the church. Why? Seek other women writers whose experience and faith are well expressed. One group could do a "women only" collection to supplement the overbalance on males. Are there particular dimensions of contemporary Christian experience which are overlooked, "Jesus people," "evangelicals," "theologians of revolution or liberation"? Are there passages that, according to your own criteria, are too sentimental or too harsh? Which? Why?

If the group wishes to make a book together, selecting the

best from each member's journal, individual stories, thoughts, and contemplations, and material gathered from other writers, this could be one of the goals for the course. If so, an editor or *editorial team* should be selected early which would gather the material at each session and present its choices for group approval at the succeeding session.

Someone talented in art or graphics could be preparing a cover for this anthology or common reader. Others can be retyping the material for the anthology. The more original the material the more interesting the book will be in matters of personal witness and contemplation, original poems, prayers, thoughts, and stories. The group may have access to a movie camera or a member may be especially talented in making color slides so that a film or slide presentation rather than a book would be the medium for the group's message. Or, your anthology can be accompanied by such illustrations. Don't forget the tape recorder here for readings, poems, songs, and dialogue.

Unless your group's study is highly personal, and individually and corporately creative, this adventure in spiritual growth will have missed its mark. It is intended to engage you in contemplation of the meaning of your belief in the Way of Jesus and in Salvation Today.

SOME QUESTIONS FOR REFLECTION

I. FAITH, HOPE, AND LOVE

1. Before doing deeper research on the writers, the group should share those passages which have spoken most directly to them. Which do not yield their meaning immediately? Do you agree with Florence Allshorn that, if the desire for self would give way into something outside ourselves, our spirit would be kindled with "ever renewing life?" Compare the definitions of love in Allshorn, Buechner, and King passages.

In "The New Being" Paul Tillich discusses reconciliation. What does he mean when he says the New Creation happens "where one is grasped by a human face as human, although one has to overcome personal distaste, or racial strangeness, or national conflicts, or the differences of sex, of age, or beauty, of strength, of knowledge, and all the other innumerable causes of separation"? Read "Easter Certainty" by Emil Brunner. How is his view of reconciliation the same as or different from Tillich's? What, according to Brunner, keeps us from reconciliation with God? Do you agree?

2. This section deals not only with expressions of belief but with some of the disciplines of the Christian life such as prayer and contemplation. Do the writers themselves differ on the meaning of prayer? Examine some of the prayers included. What are your own practices? The morning prayers of Dietrich Bonhoeffer were offered for fellow prisoners, many facing death. Florence Allshorn was the founder of St. Julian's Community where Christians today seek renewal in their Christian life through study, quiet, and common devotional practices. Discuss individual prayer and common prayer. Read *The Way of a Pilgrim,* New York: Seabury Press, 1970, a classic on the *hesychast* method of prayer, the "Jesus prayer," translated from the Russian by R. M. French.

3. What does Bonhoeffer mean by "cheap and costly grace?" Compare this with what Karl Barth says in the passage, "Who Are We Anyway?" How have you experienced the grace of God in your own life?

4. Note the sequence of the last passages in this section: Whoever We Are; Who Put the Question? Who Am I? Who He Is. What do these "who" passages have in common? Does the order of the sequence make sense to you or would another arrangement have been better?

II. WITNESS

1. Compare the statement of the RAF pilot quoted by Florence Allshorn, "Don't work for my salvation, show me yours, show me it is possible and the knowledge that something works will give me courage and belief in mine," with Berrigan's comment on "incarnational relationships" in "Style of Life."

Do you feel that you and your fellow Christians make this visible witness to Christ through your own lives? How do people become Christians today? How does witness take place?

2. In many times and places the witness of the confessing church has been oppressed or prohibited by the government. In his letter about the chestnut tree, written in a concentration camp, Paul Schneider compares the "confessing Church," which resisted Hitler while the official church went along, to the buds of a tree which he sees from his cell.

Sometimes a church which tries to witness, loses money, members, power, even freedom. Do you know of such churches? Where in our time has the church suffered because of its witness? Where has it failed to witness by going along with the prevailing political climate or accommodating itself to the values of society?

3. Compare the conversion experience of the French Jewish agnostic and intellectual Simone Weil to that of Monica Furlong who was brought up in a nominal Christian church.

Do you hear often of conversion experiences today? What does conversion mean? What does salvation mean today? Suzanne de Dietrich says Jesus wants those who experience the joy of his freedom to release others. Does this have meaning for you?

4. Witness isn't always easy. Martin Luther King tells of his struggle not to become bitter in *A Distant Lamp.* Mother Teresa addresses a prayer, entitled "Jesus My Patient," to the Lord and asks him to help her see Jesus behind the faces of the ugly, the exacting, the unreasonable. What are the obstacles to witness? Where is the help? Why does Niles speak of "grumbling to mother"?

5. Suzanne de Dietrich describes a prophet as one who does everything at the wrong time. In his *Letter From a Birmingham Jail,* Martin Luther King answers critics who ask the Negro to wait for a more convenient season. What does this say about timing and prophecy? Reinhold Niebuhr speaks of the reason that prophets are itinerants. Dan Berrigan tells why "peacemaking is hard." Is it necessary for a prophet to be an itinerant?

6. Hunger is discussed by Janet Lacey, Mother Teresa, and Dom Helder Câmara. What has this to do with witness?

7. Compare the passages of Roger Schutz, Michel Quoist, and Simone Weil on saints. What is meant by a new sanctity

or a new saintliness? What is a saint? Are saints only those who are dead?

Some Possible Assignments and Materials to Be Ordered

Order: "Salvation Today and Contemporary Experience" $1.75; "Biblical Perspectives on Salvation: A Selection of Biblical Texts with Comments," 35 cents; and "Salvation Today II." *International Review of Mission,* vol. LXI, no. 241, January 1972, $1.75 from the World Council of Churches, 475 Riverside Drive, Room 439, New York, N.Y. 10027. Order the "Salvation Today" issue of *Alive Now* from Upper Room, 1908 Grand Avenue, Nashville, Tennessee 37202 (Winter 1972 issue) 75 cents per copy, 10 or more, 50 cents each.

Study "You Are My Witnesses" by Suzanne de Dietrich, *response,* April 1973.

Order the little book *The Radical Bible* from Friendship Press* and read the passages on development, affluence, and poverty and relate them to this section. $1.95.

Order *World Update* (20 cents) which includes an interview with Dom Helder Câmara.*

Write for a copy of IDOC ($2) in which Brady Tyson, former United Methodist missionary to Brazil, discusses Dom Helder Câmara and his ministry to the poor of his land. (IDOC, No. 22, March 27, 1971; 235 East 49 Street, New York, N.Y. 10017).

Relate the Faith and Justice studies* of Friendship Press to this section.

*7820 Reading Road, Cincinnati, Ohio 45237

III. CHURCH AND WORLD

1. Some writers in this section are critical of the institutional church. Others like Barth warn us not to despise "this strange communion of strange saints." What does Barth mean when he says that if we are ashamed of the church we are inhuman where God is human and ashamed of Christ?

2. Make a list of the strengths and weaknesses of the church as described by various writers in this section. What are the sources of its strengths? Who is responsible for the weaknesses?

3. Often the church has been set against the world —

good versus evil, God versus devil. Why? Can the church live without the world? The world without the church? Explain.

4. Do you agree with Janet Lacey that "most of us do not love people"? What is she getting at? Do you agree that the kind of sentimentalists she talks about are more often to be found outside the church?

5. Melvin Schoonover says the church is the place where the love described in I Corinthians 13 is "seen, celebrated, proclaimed." Compare this with Monica Furlong's description in "Determined Masculinity" of the church as a place of pomposity and false reverence where the emotions and reality of personal life are feared. Do you agree with her diagnosis that many ills of the churches stem from a determined masculinity?

6. Read the passage on "The 60 and the 940" and follow it by using Dom Helder Câmara's prayer in the group. Do you find it possible to pray this prayer with conviction? Explain why or why not.

7. The passage, "Redemption as Power," is from the early *Notebooks of a Tamed Cynic* by the young Reinhold Niebuhr in the days of his first pastorate. What does this say to us of ordinary people and the ministry of the church and the power of the Gospel? Can you cite similar incidents where the preached word was made manifest in your life or that of someone you know?

8. In 'Israel Believed in Money" Suzanne de Dietrich calls our attention to Amos and Israel. Is our world or nation vastly different from Israel? What does this have to say to us?

9. The vow of voluntary poverty which the Brothers of Taize community try to live by is rare today. Why does Roger Schutz warn against the possibility of such voluntary poverty becoming hard? Is there any group which you know which has voluntarily sacrificed wealth for the sake of others and for Christ?

IV. LIFE AND DEATH

1. What does Tillich mean by the "new reality"? What does the knowledge of forgiveness have to do with the ability to accept and love life?

2. Buechner says perhaps God speaks to us most clearly

through his silence. But he also speaks to us about ourselves through all "the absurd little meetings, decisions, inner skirmishes that go to make up our days." Do you agree that God speaks precisely into the "nonsense of our days"? How does Buechner define real miracles?

3. Read the experiences of Claude Thompson, Masahisa Suzuki, and Joseph Mathews in encountering death. What do they have in common? How do they differ? Members of the group can be invited to undertake an assignment which they may share at a subsequent session: write of death out of your experience, describing doubt and despair, anger and assurance, or whatever thought and emotions are true to your experience. Make the narrative as vivid and true as you can.

4. Alexander Solzhenitsyn's articulation of his experience of God has sometimes brought him into trouble with the authorities of his government. Does he have an exaggerated idea of the meaning attached to military memorial days? Is the shyness and fear of death he describes peculiar to a "godless" society?

5. Suffering draws us deep into experiences of life and death. Read the passages by Schoonover, Michel Quoist, and William Stringfellow. Share your own experiences of suffering or as a witness to suffering. What does Martin Luther King mean by "redemptive suffering"? Is there anything redemptive about ordinary, capricious, unsought suffering?

6. D. T. Niles describes the search for God as "the cry of the soul for home." What does he say concerning anxiety? Compare with Tillich's comments on anxiety.

7. Discuss Thomas Merton's statement that the Christian is not concerned really with a life divided between this world and the next.

8. In "Choose Anew," Quoist says "outside of life there is no salvation." What is the meaning of this? What does *salvation today* mean? What does Tillich have to say of *salvation*? Read articles in church magazines (April 1973 issues of *response* and *new world outlook* on "Consultation on Salvation Today" held near Bangkok, Thailand, early in 1973) and write to the New York office of the World Council of Churches (475 Riverside Drive, Room 439, New York, N.Y. 10027) for the "Salvation Today" materials.

V. JOY, FREEDOM, AND PEACE

1. This section is one which is better experienced than critically examined. Litanies and liturgies, praise and prayer, song and art may yield more significant experience than questions and answers. Ask members of the sub-groups on art and Bible to share their experiences. Use the journals, poems, prayers, and posters created by the group.

2. As a group prepare a special service of celebration for the final session, using both your own prayers and litanies and any materials from this section or other parts of the book that lend themselves to corporate celebration.

3. Compare the use of dance as metaphor in passages of Merton, Kagawa, Hammarskjöld, Cox, and the Psalmists. The song "Lord of the Dance" by Sidney Carter has had wide use in congregations in recent years. Sing it. If there are dancers in the church or community who specialize in worship (Dallas and Denver are two centers of such groups), invite them to participate in this session.

4. Is the idea of laughter as a component of true religion alien to you? Why has the church been associated with solemnity? Some may wish to read and report on theologians of play (the book, *To a Dancing God* by Sam Keen, is on the 1973 Reading List). Jurgen Moltmann, the German theologian of hope, has written an interesting though sometimes difficult little book, *Theology of Play* (Harper & Row, 1972).

5. Niebuhr and Martin Luther King, Jr. speak of the American experience of the pursuit of happiness. Why are these more somber notes included here? Read *Sorrow and Joy* by Bonhoeffer and have a member of the group who has researched Bonhoeffer's life tell the experience out of which it came.

6. As the study approaches the end, recall together what it has meant to individuals and the group. Has it increased your ability to feel? To think? Does the order of the book make sense? If not, how would it have been better arranged? Have you been led to read other books by the men and women in this collection? Have you been touched by personality as well as abstract thought? Did the study lead to action as well as contemplation? If not, why? Did the group share joy, freedom, peace? Who spoke to you most deeply?

BIBLIOGRAPHY

Books in print may be ordered from the Cokesbury Book Store serving your territory, unless otherwise designated. Your local church, public and college libraries may be able to lend you books marked "out-of-print." Prices are subject to change. [Roman numerals indicate section numbers. Page numbers refer to the books quoted.]

BOOKS:

Allshorn, Florence. *The Notebooks of Florence Allshorn,* Selected and arranged by a member of St. Julian's Community (London: SCM Press, Ltd.) 1957. Out of Print.
I:54, 65-66, 80-81, 96-97; II: 14-16, 104-105.

Barth, Karl. *Deliverance To The Captives* (New York: Harper & Row) 1961. Out of Print.   I:37, 39-40.

Barth, Karl. *The Humanity of God* (Richmond, Va.: John Knox Press) 1960. $1.75.   III: 63-64.

Berrigan, Daniel, S.J. *America Is Hard to Find* (New York: Doubleday & Co.) 1972. $5.95.   II: 106-107; V: 140-141.

Berrigan, Daniel, S.J. *They Call Us Dead Men:* Reflections on Life and Conscience. Introduction by William Stringfellow. (New York: The Macmillan Co.) 1968. $1.45, paper.
I: 106-107; II: 115; III: 16-17, 182.

Bonhoeffer, Dietrich. *Letters and Papers from Prison.* (New York: The Macmillan Co.) 1967. $1.45, paper.
I: 72-74, 188-189; V: 173-175.

Bonhoeffer, Dietrich, *The Cost of Discipleship.* (New York: The Macmillan Co.) 1963. $1.95, paper.
I:41, 46, 47.

Brunner, Emil. *I Believe in the Living God,* Sermons on the Apostles' Creed, translated and edited by John Holden. (Phila.: The Westminster Press.) 1961. (Out of Print)
I: 90-93.

Buechner, Frederick. *The Alphabet of Grace.* (New York: The Seabury Press.) 1970. $3.95.
I: 3-4, 8; V: 43-46.

Buechner, Frederick. *The Magnificent Defeat.* (New York: The Seabury Press.) 1968. $1.65, paper.
I: 105, 129-130; IV: 47-50.

Cox, Harvey. *The Feast of Fools.* (New York: Harper & Row) 1970. $1.95, paper.
V: 73, 156-157.

Day, Dorothy. *A Penny a Copy.* Readings from *The Catholic Worker* edited by Thomas C. Cornell and James H. Forest (New York: The Macmillan Co.) 1968. $6.95.
II: 44-45; IV: 46-48.

Dietrich, Suzanne de. *Free Men:* Meditations on the Bible Today. Translated by Olive Wyon. (Phila.: The Westminster Press) 1961. $1.25, paper.
II:46, 51-52, 85; III: 42-43, 45; V: 17, 100-101, 105.

Furlong, Monica. *With Love to the Church.* A Forward Movement Miniature Book. (London: Hodder and Stoughton, Ltd. 1965 Order from The Forward Movement, Cincinnati, Ohio. Fifty cents.)
II: 101-104; III: 92-93, 112, 113.

Hammarskjöld, Dag. *Markings.* Translated by Leif Sjöberg and W. H. Auden (New York: Alfred A. Knopf) 1964. $5.95.
I: 100, 131, 205; V: 82-83.

Jordan, Clarence. *The Substance of Faith and Other Cotton Patch Sermons* (New York: Association Press) 1972. $4.95.
II: 73, 75, 76, 77.

Kagawa, Toyohiko. *Songs from the Slums.* Interpretation by Lois J. Erickson. Introduction by Sherwood Eddy. (Nashville: Abingdon Press) 1935. (Out of Print)
I: 46-48; V: 40-42.

King, Martin Luther, Jr. *Stride Toward Freedom:* The Montgomery Story. (New York: Harper & Row) 1958. $2.95; 75 cents, paper.
II: 138-139.

King, Martin Luther, Jr. *Why We Can't Wait.* (New York: A Signet Book published by The New American Library, Inc.) 1964. 75 cents, paper.
II: 84-85, 87-89; III: 89-90, 92.

King, Martin Luther, Jr. "A New Sense of Direction." *Worldview,* April, 1972.   V: 12.

Martin Luther King, Jr. Edited by Robert G. Hoyt. (Waukesha, Wis. Country Beautiful Foundation, Inc.) 1970. $6.95.
I: 86, 91; II: 73; IV: 82; V: 89.

Lacey, Janet. *A Cup of Water:* The Story of Christian Aid. (London: Hodder & Stoughton, Ltd.) 1970. $1.50, paper.
II: 162-163; III: 33-35, 52-54.

Mathews, Joseph W. "The Time My Father Died" (Chicago: *The Ecumenical Institute)* reprint (leaflet), 25 cents.
IV: 1, 3, 4.

Merton, Thomas. *Conjectures of a Guilty Bystander* (New York: Doubleday & Co., Inc.), Image Books edition, 1968. $1.45, paper.
IV: 233-234; V: 11-12.

Merton, Thomas. *New Seeds of Contemplation* (New York: New Directions Publishing Corp.) 1972. $2.25, paper.
I: 1-2, 37-38; IV: 26, 27, 28, 106; V: 25, 296-297.

Moosbrugger, Bernhard, and Gladys Weigner. *A Voice of The Third World:* Dom Helder Camara. (New York: Pyramid Publications, A Division of Pyramid Communications, Inc.) 1972. $1.25, paper.
II: 81, 85; III: 73, 77, 79, 109, 111, 113, 115, 116.

Muggeridge, Malcolm. *Something Beautiful for God* (Mother Teresa) (New York: Harper & Row) 1971. $5.95.
I: 52-53; II: 74-75, 76, 78-79; V: 68, 72-73.

Niebuhr, Reinhold. *Beyond Tragedy:* Essays on the Christian Interpretation of History (New York: Chas. Scribner's Sons) 1965.
$2.65, paper.
I: 168-169.

Niebuhr, Reinhold. *The Irony of American History* (New York: Chas.
Scribner's Sons) 1952. $2.45, paper.
V: 62-64.

Niebuhr, Reinhold. *Leaves from the Notebooks of a Tamed Cynic.*
(New York: The Seabury Press.) 1968. $2.75, paper.
II: 74, 75; III: 45-46; IV: 216-217.

Niles, Daniel T. *The Message and Its Messengers.* (Nashville: Abingdon Press) 1966. $2.50.
II: 26-28.

Niles, Daniel T. *That They May Have Life.* (New York: Harper & Row)
1951. Out of Print.
II: 29-30; IV: 42-43.

O'Connor, Elizabeth. *Our Many Selves.* (New York: Harper & Row)
1971. $1.95, paper.
VI: 252.

Quoist, Michel. *Christ Is Alive!* (New York: Doubleday & Co., Inc.)
Translation 1971, 1972. $1.25.
II: 35, 36, 37; IV: 86-87, 110; V: 115.

Rivers, Clarence Joseph. *Celebration.* (New York: Herder & Herder)
1968. $4.95.
V: 14, 29-30, 50.

Schneider, R. et al. *Dying We Live.* [Alfred Schmidt-Sas] (New
York: The Seabury Press.) 1968. $2.75, paper.
II: 14-15; IV: 176, 178, 179.

Schoonover, Melvin E. *Letters to Polly:* On the Gift of Affliction.
(Grand Rapids, Mich.: William B. Eerdmans Publishing Co.) 1971.
$3.95.
III: 42-43; IV: 105-106.

Schutz, Roger. *The Power of the Provisional.* (Boston: Pilgrim Press)
Trans 1969. (London: Hodder & Stoughton, Ltd.). Out of Print.
III: 31-33.

Schutz, Roger. *Unity Man's Tomorrow.* (New York: Herder &
Herder) 1963. Out of Print.   I: 93-94; II: 77-78.

Schweitzer, Albert. *The Quest of the Historical Jesus.* (New York:
The Macmillan Co.) 1968. $3.95, paper.   I: 403.

Solzhenitsyn, Alexander. *Stories and Prose Poems.* (New York:
Farrar, Straus & Giroux, Inc.) 1971. $1.50, pa. IV: 217-218; V: 197.

Stringfellow, William. *A Second Birthday.* (New York: Doubleday &
Co., Inc.) 1970. $5.95.   IV: 97-98, 167-171.

Suzuki, Masahisa. Moderator Suzuki's Last Message. Translated by
Ian MacLeod from *Kyodan Times.*   IV: July 19, 1969.

Thompson, Claude. "How Do You Want to Die?" *Christian Advocate,* Feb. 17, 1972.   IV: 9, 10, 11.

Tillich, Paul. *The Courage to Be.* Yale Terry Lectures (New Haven: Yale University Press) 1952. $2.25, paper.   I: 171-172, 180-181.

Tillich, Paul. *The New Being.* (New York: Chas. Scribner's Sons) 1955. $1.95, paper.   I: 20-24; II: 26-29; IV: 10-14, 40-42.

Weil, Simone. *Waiting for God.* Trans. Emma Craufurd. (New York: Harper & Row) 1973. $1.95, paper.   II: 99.

ABOUT THE AUTHOR

A native of Georgia, Betty Thompson was educated at Wesleyan College, Macon, Ga. (A.B., *cum laude).* She did graduate work in literary criticism at the Kenyon School of English in Gambier, Ohio. While in college, Miss Thompson wrote for the *Macon Telegraph* and *Atlanta Journal.* For two years she was public relations director at Wesleyan. Her first job in New York was as staff writer for the Methodist Board of Missions. For nearly a decade, she was an information officer for the World Council of Churches, first in Geneva, Switzerland, and then in New York. Since 1965, she has headed the communications unit of the United Methodist Board of Global Ministries.

Turning World, her account of a global ecumenical journey, was published by Friendship Press in 1960. An essay on the American writer Thomas Wolfe has been published in two anthologies. Her articles and stories have been published in all parts of the world. Miss Thompson worked on the press staff at major ecumenical conferences such as the World Council of Churches assemblies in New Delhi, India and Uppsala, Sweden, and at meetings in Mexico City and Montreal.

The first woman to be elected an editor-at-large of the *Christian Century,* Miss Thompson frequently covers ecumenical and United Methodist events for that journal. She has served as correspondent for Religious News Service, most recently at the World Consultation on "Salvation Today," at Bangkok, Thailand. She is on the advisory communications committee of both the National and World Councils of Churches. In 1970, Wesleyan College honored her with its distinguished achievement award.

THE HEALING FOUNTAIN

Prepared by the Education and Cultivation Division
Board of Global Ministries • The United Methodist Church

SERVICE CENTER
7820 Reading Road • Cincinnati, Ohio 45237
Price $1.45

FE473